## ADVANCED PRAISE FOR
### *THE DIARY OF DUKESANG WONG*

"This book is like no other. Dukesang Wong's diary provides unparalleled insights into the experiences and perceptions of the earliest Chinese immigrants to Canada's Pacific province. If you are at all interested in the complex situations that motivated Chinese men to leave their homeland, and their challenging experiences upon arriving and building new lives in Canada, this book is a must read."

> —**Keith Thor Carlson**, Canada Research Chair in Indigenous and Community-Engaged History, University of the Fraser Valley

"These are words that make real the raw racism and brutal life struggles faced by workers on the CPR. Wong's diary narrates a captivating journey through time, sprinkled with major world events. A must read for anyone who's ever wondered how nineteenth-century people of colour experienced North America."

> —**David H.T. Wong**, architect and author

# The Diary of Dukesang Wong

# The Diary of Dukesang Wong

**A VOICE FROM GOLD MOUNTAIN**

## Dukesang Wong

Edited with commentary by David McIlwraith
Diary translated by Wanda Joy Hoe
Introduction by Judy Fong Bates

Talonbooks

Talonbooks
9259 Shaughnessy Street, Vancouver, British Columbia, Canada V6P 6R4
talonbooks.com

Talonbooks is located on xʷməθkʷəy̓əm, Sḵwx̱wú7mesh, and səl̓ilwətaʔɬ Lands.

First printing: 2020

Typeset in Minion
Printed and bound in Canada on 100% post-consumer recycled paper

Cover design by Typesmith, interior design by andrea bennett
Cover photo courtesy of Victor Calvin Hoe

Talonbooks acknowledges the financial support of the Canada Council for the Arts, the Government of Canada through the Canada Book Fund, and the Province of British Columbia through the British Columbia Arts Council and the Book Publishing Tax Credit.

LIBRARY AND ARCHIVES CANADA CATALOGUING IN PUBLICATION

Title: The diary of Dukesang Wong : a voice from Gold Mountain / Dukesang Wong ; edited with commentary by David McIlwraith ; diary translated by Wanda Joy Hoe ; introduction by Judy Fong Bates.
Other titles: Diaries. Selections. English
Names: Wong, Dukesang, 1845– author. | McIlwraith, David, editor, writer of added commentary. | Hoe, Wanda Joy, 1947– translator. | Bates, Judy Fong, 1949– writer of introduction.
Description: Includes bibliographical references. | Diary entries translated from the Chinese.
Identifiers: Canadiana 20200256009 | ISBN 9781772012583 (SOFTCOVER)
Subjects: LCSH: Wong, Dukesang, 1845-–Diaries. | LCSH: Canadian Pacific Railway Company—Employees—Diaries. | LCSH: Chinese—British Columbia—Diaries. | LCSH: Railroad construction workers—British Columbia—Diaries. | LCSH: Chinese—British Columbia—Social conditions—19th century. | LCGFT: Diaries.
Classification: LCC FC3850.C5 W66 2020 | DDC 971.1/0049510092—dc23

*To the faces not in the picture*

*So very difficult a matter it is to trace and find
out the truth of anything by history.*

—PLUTARCH, *PARALLEL LIVES*

# The Diary of Dukesang Wong

# Foreword

I grew up listening to stories about a man I never met. My mother, my grandmother, and my uncles sat around our kitchen table and talked about my maternal grandfather every time they gathered at our house. He had died sixteen years before I was born, but still they talked about his journey from China to North America, his time working on the railway, the many roles he played in our Chinese Canadian community, and his passion for and commitment to education. And they talked about notebooks he had written, diaries that told the story of his life. They also talked about the struggles the family faced in being accepted into North American society. My grandmother told the story of being allowed to clean the church down the road, but not to attend it because she was Chinese.

A few years later, still fascinated by all these stories, I wrote a paper for a professor at Simon Fraser University. Included in the paper were excerpts taken from my grandfather's notebooks, translations I had made with help from my uncles Charlie and Dan. I got an A on the paper, but after I put it away in a box, I never imagined it would have a life beyond my sociology class. All these years later, I am delighted that my grandfather's voice will be heard again.

—WANDA JOY HOE
Ottawa, Ontario
February 2020

# Introduction

When I first saw the photographs of the Last Spike, commemorating the completion of the Canadian Pacific Railway, I was in either grade five or six. The teacher stood at the front of the class and told the students, all sitting in tidy rows of wooden desks, about the importance of that moment, how Canada was then united and became a country. As I looked at those historic photos, I knew even then that the men in the centre of the group were important. They were the decision makers. They were powerful and rich. And they were white.

It wasn't until I was a young adult that I learned about the role of the Chinese in the building of that railway, especially the western portion through the mountains of British Columbia. Ever since I realized the contribution by Chinese labour, such photographs took on new meaning for me. The absence of the Chinese in those photos has become symbolic of our role in Canada's story. We are defined by our absence.

The role of the Chinese in the building of Canadian society existed for many years in the margins. It has only been during the last two or three decades that the children and grandchildren of those early immigrants have started to investigate and imagine their stories. The journey out of the shadows and into the light of mainstream Canadian history continues for the Chinese. There are now archives in Vancouver and in Toronto that are devoted to the history of the Chinese in Canada. Chinese artists, writers, and filmmakers have started telling our stories. Yet our acceptance into established Canadian society can feel still tenuous. At this moment of writing, the coronavirus pandemic has gripped Canada and the world. With the virus originating in China, there have been unfortunate attacks against Chinese who live in Canada, some whose families have been here for many generations and who have never been to China. For many years I had been lulled into thinking that although acts of racism against the Chinese were relatively few, by and large we belonged in Canadian society. As a group we have been in Canada for more than a century. Chinese men enlisted in the military and fought for Canada in the last World War. We had transformed ourselves from being unwanted and despised to being the "model minority." But recent events tell me that our journey is far from over.

In 1955, when I was five years old, my mother and I left China and arrived in a small town outside of Toronto to join my father in his hand laundry. I was the only child of colour in our small town, and my mother was the only non-white woman. Everyone at my school and probably in the entire town knew who I was. My father washed other people's clothes, and I was known as the "little Chinese girl." My entire world was white: my friends, my teachers, the fireman, the policeman, the lawyer, the man who owned the hardware store. The people in the books I read were white. And with the exception of Hop Sing in *Bonanza* and Peter in *Bachelor Father*, there were no Chinese people on television. My notions of beauty and sexuality were all based on the white society in which I lived. Nowhere did I see myself. Nowhere was I validated. In my dreams the boys were handsome and white, and I had blue eyes and golden hair flowed down my back.

I had wonderful teachers who taught me many things. I learned how Canada was "discovered" and settled by Europeans. I learned about totem poles and teepees, log houses and corduroy roads. I learned about the kings and queens of England. I learned about important people like Samuel de Champlain, John Cabot, John A. Macdonald, Wilfrid Laurier. I even learned about the American, French, and Russian Revolutions, German unification under Bismarck. But I learned next to nothing about China, India, Iran, Ghana, Uganda, Brazil, Argentina, Chile. It seemed that anything of historical consequence belonged to the west, anything of note that was accomplished in Canada was accomplished by people who were white and European. No one told me about the role of the Chinese in the building of the railroad, or the *Komagata Maru*, or the internment of the Japanese during World War II.

I was never told that people who looked like me had no real role in the development of this country. But our absence from the story spoke volumes. In fact, we were unwanted, something about which my father routinely reminded me. He told me about having to pay a head tax in 1914 in order to enter Canada. Five hundred dollars! Only the Chinese were made to pay. He would ask, "Do you know what I could have bought with that much money back then?" And like a dutiful daughter, I listened. But when I went to school, the things that my parents told me faded into insignificance compared to the things that I learned in my class. What I learned at school were the important things, because they came out of the mouths of my teachers, were in books, broadcast on television, written about in newspapers. The unintentional result of growing up in an environment where I was such a small minority was that whatever points of view my parents presented were overshadowed, somehow considered less worthy and perhaps even erroneous.

One example that sticks in my mind is that at school I learned that World War II lasted six years. It started in 1939 and ended in 1945. But according to my parents that war lasted eight years. In my young mind I just assumed that they must be wrong. The war lasted six years. It was there in black and white in textbooks, in newspapers. The teachers, the Canadians who fought in the War, all said it was six years. Obviously, my parents were wrong, or they just couldn't add. But as I grew older and started to read further and think more for myself, I began to realize that history, in fact, has many points of view. The war for my parents started in 1937 with the invasion of China by the Japanese and ended in 1945. For them it added up to eight years. They were right. I was almost middle-aged when I realized that an absent point of view was not necessarily an invalid one. As I look back, I realize that for more than half of the twentieth century, the Chinese, although considered a "visible" minority in Canada, were, in fact, invisible, for everywhere I looked in the Canadian cultural landscape we were not there. A few people had broken through – Normie Kwong, Adrienne Clarkson – but by and large we were invisible.

When I was sixteen, a schoolmate introduced me to the work of James Baldwin. Even though I understood very little, I devoured *Another Country* and *Giovanni's Room*. Until then all the books I had read were by people who were white. But here was a man who was Black and wrote books which people bought and read. Unbeknownst to me a notion was planted in my head: that I too might have stories to share, that one day people might be interested in reading them. It took another thirty years for that thought to be realized. And I have David McIlwraith to thank for lending me those books by James Baldwin.

After high school I didn't see David for almost forty-five years. In the fall of 2010, I was at the University of British Columbia, giving a talk related to my family memoir, *The Year of Finding Memory*. David was in the audience. Ten years later he was in touch again, this time to ask if I would write an introduction to a book that he was editing. It was about a Chinese man during the building of the Canadian Pacific Railway. The first question that occurred to me was: Why would someone like David McIlwraith, who grew up as a member of mainstream society during the fifties and sixties, be interested in the Chinese and the Canadian railway? I later learned that David had spent many years living in British Columbia, where he developed an interest in the history of the Chinese in Canada. This interest intensified when he later adopted a daughter from China.

In 1965 David and I were in the same math class. At the time the story of the Chinese in Canada was probably the furthest thing from each of our minds. I was desperately trying to fit in, and David was likely preoccupied by his leading role in *West Side Story*. But more than fifty years later, it would be this interest that would connect us.

David's quest to learn about the history of the Chinese in Canada took him to libraries and museums in large cities and the small towns located along the CPR in British Columbia. He even returned to China a second time to visit the Four Counties, the region which was home to most of the early Chinese in Canada. But more than anything else, David wanted to find something written by someone who had been there during the building of the railway. He realized that the likelihood of anything surviving was low. If he could just find one first-hand voice. He was persistent. One day, while researching in a Fraser Valley museum, he opened an unmarked drawer in a cabinet. There he found "a single sheet of paper on which was written a translation of a two-line quote attributed to a Chinese man named Dukesang Wong" who worked on the railway in the 1880s. Ultimately this led to Wanda Joy Hoe, Dukesang Wong's granddaughter, who was able to provide David with more of her grandfather's writing.

After many years of research and work, and with the help of Wanda Joy Hoe, David has edited the diaries of Dukesang Wong, and now we are able to hear his voice. While Dukesang Wong worked on the railway, he was likely viewed by his bosses and the general public as a part of the yellow mass of faceless men who were hired as cheap and dispensable labour in order to complete the railroad. His diaries give him back his humanity and his individuality. He tells us about the harsh working conditions, the hardships, injustices, and sorrows endured, hopes and aspirations, the support of community, and the joy of family. It is a heartbreaking, but ultimately hopeful, voice that reaches out beyond the century.

By publishing Dukesang Wong's diaries, David McIlwraith has made a real contribution to the story of the Chinese in Canada. Let us hope these diaries allow us to hear Dukesang Wong's own voice and thus remind us, immigrants old and new, that we all have a role in shaping this land called Canada.

—JUDY FONG BATES
Campbellford, Ontario
May 2020

# The Diary of Dukesang Wong

# COMMENTARY: LOST AND FORGOTTEN

In the spring of the year 1867, in a Chinese village a long day's journey north from the capital city, a local family hosted a banquet. In all likelihood, the regional magistrate, an officer of the Imperial Court, was given the place of honour at the banquet table. As if his position in the community were not reason enough for the seat of honour, just a few days earlier he had ruled in favour of his host in a land dispute. Though the beginnings of a breakdown in civil order were seen to be spreading throughout China in the aftermath of the Opium Wars and the ongoing rebellions, appointees of the Emperor's Court still had authority and were generally treated with deference and respect. The magistrate couldn't possibly have suspected that the food set before him that night would be laced with arsenic and that he would die before the sun rose the next morning.

The magistrate's only son was twenty-one years old that spring. He was deeply affected by his father's death. In the days and weeks following the poisoning, he began to keep a diary, a record of his grief and confusion during a tragic time in his young life. He would continue to keep the diary, through tragedy and triumph, for five more decades. For over fifty years, Dukesang Wong made compelling and eloquent entries in his notebooks, first about his life as a young man in Imperial China and then about the life he went on to live half a world away on a continent he called the "Land of the Golden Mountains." Little did he know that more than one hundred and fifty years later, his diary would become the only primary source, the only known voice, for thousands of his generation.

Dukesang Wong was one of millions of Chinese men who emigrated from their homeland to escape war, rebellion, famine, and poverty in the latter half of the nineteenth century. Buoyed by exaggerated stories of gold nuggets to be scooped off the ground in places with names like New Zealand and America, they travelled to every corner of the globe. So alluring was the prospect of financial reward, and even of possible fortune to be found, that they called the western regions of North America "Gum Saan": "Gold Mountain."

A few thousand left China for Gum Saan as early as 1849, first to the California Gold Rush, and then in 1858 to the Fraser River Gold Rush in British Columbia, Canada. Then – even as the gold was depleted – worsening conditions in China continued to sustain the draw of Gold Mountain. In California in 1865, the first fifty Chinese workers were hired by the Central Pacific Railroad. By 1869, more than ten thousand had blasted and built a rail line through the Sierra Nevada Mountains. A decade later, the Chinese agents working on behalf of the Canadian transcontinental railway were still selling the get-rich dream, and Chinese men were still buying it. Between 1850 and 1885, tens of thousands of Chinese men came to the United States and Canada to pan for elusive gold and build transcontinental railways across both countries.[1]

First-person accounts of the Chinese workers who built railways across the North American continent are not supposed to exist. Canadian historian Pierre Berton wrote in *The Last Spike*, published in 1971, that "such details were not set down and so are lost forever – lost and forgotten, like the crumbling bones that lie in unmarked graves."[2] In a May 2019 *New York Times* piece, American historian Andrew Graybill wrote that "the lived experience of the Railroad Chinese has long been elusive, partly because no sources written in their own hand survive."[3] The notion that no primary sources exist because no one ever set words to paper – or that whatever was written had all been lost – seemed unlikely to me.

---

1    Lynn Pan, ed., *The Encyclopedia of the Chinese Overseas* (Cambridge, MA: Harvard University Press, 1998).

2    Pierre Berton, *The Last Spike: The Great Railway, 1881–1885* (Toronto: Anchor Canada, 1971), 205.

3    Andrew Graybill, "The Forgotten History of the Chinese Who Helped Build America's Railroads," *New York Times*, May 10, 2019, www.nytimes .com/2019/05/10/books/review/gordon-h-chang-ghosts-of-gold -mountain.html.

Surely there had to be written accounts, primary sources of some type hiding forgotten in someone's attic. It was that surety that propelled a lengthy and stubborn search.

Twentieth-century histories of the building of the transcontinental railways in North America usually devoted very few pages to the thousands of Chinese workers who built significant portions of those rail lines through the American West and through Canada's treacherous Fraser Canyon. Nevertheless, the histories were intriguing, not least because they revealed so little about the workers. Most often there were no names included, few anecdotes about any one of them, and little about what they did, other than to say they worked at the dirty and dangerous jobs or that so very many of them died. Why the blank space in our histories? The stories told and taught for a hundred years across North America have largely been stories of nameless people. Perhaps that was the fate of most working men and women in the nineteenth century. But we now know that the story of the Chinese in Gold Mountain is a very different story from all the others who voluntarily crossed oceans to the shores of this continent.

The great majority of Chinese workers who chose to come to North America in the middle of the nineteenth century, and those who made the same choice as late as the 1880s, were from the southern provinces of Guangdong and Fujian. Many of these men were illiterate, and most were subsistence farmers barely surviving one year to the next through famine and drought. But some, like Dukesang Wong, arrived from other parts of China, and not all who came left their homes in desperation. And of course not all who came, regardless of where in China they came from, were illiterate. Among the thousands landing at ports from Victoria to San Francisco were herbalists, tailors, scribes, and teachers. Most came for the same reason, to make some much-needed money to send back to China, or to take back with them when the work was done. Others came believing they could make a new life for themselves in Gold Mountain.

In the official stories of nation building on this continent, Chinese Canadians and Chinese Americans have largely been absent, and where they are acknowledged to have played a role, many of the details seemed better left unsaid. Yes, they moved rock out of the paths of rail lines and out of the tunnels of mines, they operated laundries and cut timber, they gutted fish and turned deserts into market gardens, but their stories were only grudgingly woven into the national historical fabric of countries to which they came. It is certainly true that authentic records of any kind are often difficult to find. But pervasive myths tend to dissuade the searcher: the Chinese were illiterate, the Chinese didn't keep diaries, their diaries could not have survived the decades, it was all destroyed in the Cultural Revolution, and so on.

A more accurate explanation for the perceived lack of primary sources might be that the racism and violence directed at Chinese immigrants in the United States and Canada throughout much of the nineteenth and twentieth centuries included erasing them, both from the landscape and from history. On November 3, 1885, in Tacoma, Washington, two hundred Chinese men and woman were driven out of the city by a mob of hundreds of "upstanding" citizens, including the mayor and local judges. These men and women were forced to walk a few miles to a small railway station, spend the night standing in the rain, board a train the next morning, and leave the state. The next day the homes and businesses of their Chinatown, along with the contents of those buildings, were burned to the ground. Not a doorframe remained. The event became known as the "Tacoma Method."[4] Seen as a highly effective way to rid the community of Chinese people, the method was copied in towns and cities spread throughout western North America.[5]

The Chinese were attacked, killed, and driven out of towns up and down the continent. Their Chinatowns were torn down, burned down, and forgotten all the way from California to British Columbia. Their contributions were ignored and dismissed. In both countries, a visit to most of those towns today, which for many years had large and even majority Chinese-born populations, will reveal nothing to remind the visitor that the Chinese were ever there. Is it any wonder that records and personal accounts are hard to find? As a result of these attitudes and actions, the thousands of Chinese who gave their labour, and the hundreds who gave their lives to the nation-building projects of North America, have been denied their rightful place in its history.

Yet history reveals itself in many and sometimes surprising ways. Time and again our histories are altered when new evidence appears.

---

4   Chinese Reconciliation Project Foundation (website), "Expulsion: The Tacoma Method," www.tacomachinesepark.org/tacoma-chinese-park /expulsion-the-tacoma-method/.

5   Peter Kwong and Dušanka Miščević, *Chinese America: The Untold Story of America's Oldest New Community* (New York: New Press, 2007).

And it does appear, despite the efforts to erase it. The diaries of Dukesang Wong, and those of the labour-recruiting agent Ah Quin, held today in the San Diego Archives, were both recovered recently.[6] There is every probability that there is more to come.

In 1996, Canadian ethnohistorian Keith Thor Carlson was researching the 1884 lynching of an Indigenous boy in British Columbia's Fraser Valley, the traditional territory of the Stó:lō First Nation. Reading through documents from the period in the BC Archives, Carlson came across a police report about the lynching which included a disturbing quote. One of the members of the lynch mob was reported to have said, "I'd kill a Chinaman as quick as I would an Indian and I'd kill an Indian as quick as I would a dog."[7]

The history of white settler racism in North America doesn't come as a surprise in the twenty-first century. We've long known about the genocide perpetrated against the Indigenous Peoples of the continent, the lynching of thousands of African Americans, and the racist loathing of the Chinese. Yet even in the context of this hate-filled history, it's still shocking to hear the ease with which settlers imagined killing anyone who didn't look like them and didn't share their culture.

I made my first visit to China a few years before reading that terrible quote, travelling with my partner first to Beijing, then on to the city of Luoyang in north-central China. We had travelled to this former capital city of ancient China to adopt our daughter. It was a trip that profoundly and joyfully changed our lives, and intimately connected us to a land we had only imagined, a country and a people whose storied history spans an almost unbroken five thousand years, the oldest living civilization on earth. Those first days together in China are etched forever in our memories.

---

6   The Ah Quin diary collection contains ten small pocket-size booklets.
    The first was begun in 1876 in Alaska, where he worked for a year as
    cook at a mining site. After returning to California, he served as a
    servant and cook until 1880, when he began work as a labour broker
    in San Diego for the California Southern Railroad. The diaries were
    donated to the San Diego Histrical Society by Ah Quin's descendants.

7   Keith Thor Carlson, "The Lynching of Louie Sam," *BC Studies* 109
    (Spring 1996), ojs.library.ubc.ca/index.php/bcstudies/article/view/1309.

As we stepped off the airplane back home in Canada, our daughter in my arms, my interest in the history of the Chinese in North America, initiated years before with Berton's *The Last Spike*, had grown to become the heart of the work I went on to do for several years, made all the more determined by the hundred-year-old words of a lynch-mob killer. The first stage of my work was the search, a search based on the conviction that I would be able to find what so many said did not exist.

This attempt to shed new light on an obscured part of our continental history needed original voices, someone's long-forgotten notebooks or letters. I began the search for such a voice with a second trip to China. A few thousand men had returned home after their "sojourn" in Gold Mountain, and I hoped to find something there, especially in the region once called the Siyi, the four counties in the south of Guangdong Province, from which a vast majority of the men had migrated. I searched in cities and villages like Taishan, Baisha, and Kaiping. I visited the Jiangmen Wuyi Museum of Overseas Chinese, where I was shown artifacts brought back to China more than a century before from places like Portland, Oregon and Ashcroft, British Columbia; from cities and towns in Australia and New Zealand; from Southeast Asia; and from South America.

There were landing permits, employment contracts, English-language picture books, American-made tools, accounting ledgers, and letters, some of greeting and many of instruction on how remitted funds should be divided, in notes often written by scribes for the many men who could neither read nor write. Chinese scholars warned that some of the letters written home may not have been entirely reliable, that writers would have spared loved ones the disturbing details of their difficult lives abroad. In any event, I found no diaries or journals or even packets of letters describing details of daily life in Gold Mountain. I had assumed the best place to look was China, and that could still turn out to be true. But at the time, I began to question my conviction that something would surely turn up. However, there was another place I wanted to look, and it was much closer to home.

After returning from Guangdong without the hoped-for documents, I turned my attention to searching in Canada. Like the towns of the southern Chinese province, many communities in southern British Columbia have local museums. With help from Bev Kennedy, a former curator in one such museum, we began visiting them, some as small as one or two little rooms, in towns and villages like Yale and Agassiz and

Lytton. In one of the museums, in an unmarked drawer of an old cabinet, we found a single sheet of paper on which was written a two-line quote attributed to a diary written by a man named Dukesang Wong. The page also attributed the translation to the man's granddaughter, who years before had attended nearby Simon Fraser University. The actual diary quote made reference to working on railway construction in the 1880s. It was the most promising clue we had yet come across.

A spokesperson at the university named on the page explained that they could not give out information on former students. However, the university alumni association was more forthcoming, confirming that a former student by that name was a member of the association. Although they, too, refused to give out any more information, they found the subject intriguing and offered to contact her and pass along some details of our interest, allowing her to decide whether to make contact. A few days later, she called.

Her name was Wanda Joy Hoe, and she was living in Ottawa, 3,500 kilometres from my home in Vancouver. She explained that the quote we had found was from a selective translation of her grandfather's diaries, which she had done for an SFU assignment in 1966–1967. The original diaries had been written between 1867 and 1918, both in China and Canada. They included the period between 1881 and 1886 when her grandfather worked on the construction of Canada's transcontinental rail line, the Canadian Pacific Railway (CPR). A few days after the call, I was flying across Canada. When I arrived at her home, we quickly began looking through cardboard boxes of files and papers kept in her garage. From one of the boxes we pulled fifty-nine typewritten, mimeographed pages with the title page "A Chinese Transition to Canada."

As I sat in Wanda Joy's living room reading through the pages of her forty-two-year-old undergraduate sociology assignment, I realized I was holding a unique and very rare contribution to the histories of both China and North America. However, there are a couple of disappointments in the story that follows. The most disheartening was learning that the original handwritten diaries, seven notebooks in total, were lost in a fire a few years after the translations were made. Tragically, they had never been donated to a museum or an archive, never copied or photographed or filmed. Nevertheless, Wanda Joy's translations survived, and I had the good fortune to sit in her home on that first day of our friendship reading her translated pages and listening to her story.

Wanda Joy's mother, Elsie, was the last of eight children and the only girl in Dukesang Wong's family. Dukesang died in 1931, thirteen years after she was born. Wanda Joy was born in 1947. Although her grandfather had died years before her birth, he was often talked about in her family home. One of the subjects discussed was the diary he had kept – seven notebooks, no longer in the family's possession. They were held by the local Wong Association, one of the many clan associations common in North American cities, and the one to which Wong had once belonged. Years later, in 1966, Wanda Joy was enrolled as a charter student at Simon Fraser University near Vancouver. When she told her professor, the renowned Marxist scholar and sociologist Tom Bottomore about the diary, he proposed that she use her grandfather's writings as the core element of a course assignment.

Wanda Joy borrowed the diaries, and with help from her uncles Charlie and Dan, sons of Dukesang, she translated selected portions as they related to the theme of her paper, "A Chinese Transition to Canada." The translations were accompanied by notes to help clarify questions of family and cultural history. The entries she chose to translate constituted a reduced but remarkable selection from the diaries her grandfather had kept for five decades. After she completed her work, she returned the original notebooks to the clan office, where they were subsequently lost in a building fire. To compound this tragedy, the reel-to-reel tapes onto which her uncle Dan had read the diaries were thrown out after his death. Fortunately, though, Wanda Joy's university assignment was still in a cardboard box in her garage more than forty years after she wrote it.

The writings of Dukesang Wong were influenced by his classical education in Confucian philosophy and Chinese literature. This form of education for the sons of the elite, including the examinations they were required to write, had existed since the sixth century. It determined the fortunes of families for more than 1,400 years. These influences also shaped Wong's literary style and even the particular script in which he wrote. In writing her assignment, Wanda Joy's principal concern was family history and her grandparents' transition from a Chinese life to a North American one. The choices she made, the excerpts she chose to translate, usually reflected that theme. One of her uncles had some familiarity with his father's script and helped with transcribing the writings.

While the original style may have contributed to interesting anachronistic flourishes in the translating, it made for fascinating reading, producing quotes rich with philosophical and poetic musings and filled with details of his life and the lives of his co-workers and acquaintances, including warlords, railway workers, missionaries, and the founding leader of post-Imperial China, Dr. Sun Yat-sen. It is writing that makes us mourn the permanent loss of the many untranslated sections of those diaries. No one is more aware of this loss than Wanda Joy. But in her circumstance, she had to make choices for a single university assignment, not for a history of the Chinese in Gold Mountain. Nevertheless, what she did translate and record has made a significant contribution to that history.

The question of whether the English translations made by his granddaughter and her two uncles accurately reflect Wong's intended meanings is now moot. We can only assume that the translations were made out of a loving commitment to family, with an equal commitment to truth and accuracy. This is not to suggest, however, that they are always completely reliable. In matters of personal family history, the details may occasionally have been influenced by what was not written down or spoken of over family meals. Wanda Joy has acknowledged that there were subjects never broached in her family, details of family history considered better left unsaid; it's possible that occasional details from the original diary may have been omitted for that reason. Also, very few of the entries were accompanied by dates; some dates were guessed at by her uncles, while other details came from her grandmother, who was well into her eighties when the translations were being made in 1966/1967. As we will see, these influences, omissions, and date miscalculations will create occasional questions about chronology, but according to both family history and my own research, they do not misrepresent the narrative.

The diary entries occasionally provide specific details, but more often they don't. When they don't, they usually give us enough clues to root out a story and expand the details ourselves. I have tried to do that in the commentary whenever possible. I have also made every possible effort to explain obscure or confusing references. Wong's family members, whether sons, sisters or uncles, are identified by the traditional numbering of birth order rather than by name. For example, Wong's son, known as Uncle Dan to Wanda Joy, is only ever referred to as Second Son in the diary. Many of the names of historical figures in the 1966 diary translation predated the use of the Pinyin Romanization system among most Chinese diasporic communities. The United Nations adopted Pinyin as the standard for transliterating Standard Chinese in 1986. I've therefore kept the earlier Wade-Giles spellings as written and include the more contemporary Pinyin spellings in the commentary and notes. Some of the wording in the diaries is considered offensive today, but there were few alternatives in the 1880s. Wong used "Indian" to refer to Indigenous Peoples, for example, as does the original translation, which we use here. Similarly, social relations in nineteenth-century China were defined by now unacceptable patriarchal views of women and marriage. Colonial place names such as Peiping and Canton were also commonly used at that time, referring of course to Beijing and Guangdong/Guangzhou. There is certainly some conjecture in the commentary when unequivocal certainty, by way of family history or by research, is impossible. Those moments of guesswork are identified.

Nothing significant about Dukesang Wong's life in North America entered the official record. His name never appeared in a newspaper or a court filing. Little to nothing is known publicly about him, and only a few of his descendants know the details of his life. None of the usual sources provide information except – and this is a crucial exception – his granddaughter's university assignment and the translation of selected portions of his diary. Almost a hundred years after his death, we now appreciate how significant that translation is. For all his anonymity, he is now a singular voice for tens of thousands of men and women who played a major but too often unacknowledged role in transforming a continent.

# The China Diary

# SWEET NATIVE LAND

## Late Spring and Summer 1867

Some time has passed since my father's death, yet we must continue to mourn him. He was a greatly respected man and to die so, without honour, also leaves my life dishonoured and empty. These weeks of silence offend me and stifle my mind, because while mourning, I must neither read nor ponder philosophical thoughts. I must continually remember only him. But I can only remember the black nails of his fingers and they torment my sleep. It is certainly in the order of one's life to die, but I am also certain, not in the manner in which he died.

*

I cannot forget his good deeds, and as he instructed, I must never forget my ancestors. But the disgrace I feel at this time overcomes the necessary remembrance of the good. My mother will not come out of her quarters, and I am not allowed to enter them. I despise the duties required by this fate, and I should also despise the man who caused it. Yet I cannot despise the man even though I am my father's son.

Why is this happening? My father's name must be honoured if I am his son.

*

These things cannot be happening. The village people have taken the glorious banner of my father, and the officials have left us without a home. My mother has gone to her retreat, and I was only now informed of it. This is the end for us. This is a violent, passionate act which I never thought would, or indeed could, happen. What am I to learn from this? I cannot visit my unhappy mother in this state of turmoil. How am I to show my face anywhere?

*

My master has not come back to the village for nearly three weeks, and no one here will give me shelter. It appears I will never complete the examinations even though I am well versed in the books for my second degree. Chan[8] is trying to reach the master for me.

My life is not to be envied. I do not understand why people appear so bad. Surely there is some good still existing in them. My dear friend who is honoured at the courts has gone to Peiping to try again to influence the mandarins who can clear my father's name of the indignity and slander brought upon it.

---

8   Chan was a friend who remained loyal after the magistrate's death. He is mentioned again several years later, contemplating emigrating from China with Wong.

## Early Autumn 1867

There is no hope of ever bringing my father's name into honour again. Hoong Sei Cheong[9] has returned bearing no good news. In Peiping, they are indifferent to his attempt to re-establish my father's honoured place. The courts are preoccupied with another disturbance in the order of society, as Sun Tang[10] has regained his influence. No one will consider appeals from this house.

Perhaps I will try again next year as, according to the predictions of the master, the land will be more abundant. It will be the sixth year, and as it is said, the sixth is most profitable followed by deprivation in the seventh. It is to be hoped that the elders will hear our case then with better attitudes.

## Autumn 1867

Word has reached me of my mother's anguished lunacy. She has unbound her feet and sometimes wails in her quarters. Sun Tang has further aggravated her agonies, and she will be overwhelmed when she hears. If only I could help her, if only I could be allowed to visit her. Perhaps then I would know how to talk with her. Chan believes that the best course is to leave her to her own expressions. But such expressions! They do not honour her family. Third Uncle

---

9   Hoong Sei Cheong was another friend from the village who had connections in Beijing.
10  Sun Tang is unidentified, but seems to have been an official of the Imperial court with whom the Wong family had strained relations.

remains with her to see to her health, but no medicine can be obtained for this illness. In these empty days, medicine is not to be obtained at all.

I would wish respected Third Uncle would not act so much on her behalf while she wills her own end. He expresses too much concern, and soon the esteem for his good name will also be lost. He should also respect her wishes and express only his kind regard for her. She is much older than he, in years and in experience – my dejected mother now has a thousand years of experience. If only I could reverse them.

## Early Winter 1867

The master has returned. His absence was not a reflection of any feelings of disgrace or contempt at the accusation of dishonour to my father. He had gone to mourn his cousin's death and sympathizes with me. He has resumed his learned tutoring, though he questions whether I will even be heard once I am ready to take the examinations. Perhaps when I have proved myself and demonstrate my knowledge at the appropriate level, the courts will gladly hear my father's name again. Tai Tsa Mun, the respected leader of the scholars, will be at least sympathetic with my master's recommendation. He taught the master in his first degree.

The days have grown so very short and the light here is precious, to be frugally guarded. My mother has advised me to leave the village and move to another area, but to leave these lands at this moment is beyond my emotional stamina. Father has yet to be finally buried, and there are burial feasts to be arranged, though this is exceedingly difficult to undertake without enough money.

I am surprised that some people in this village are willing to help, but accepting their offers would be accepting help from people outside the family. Father always disliked such charity. "To help ourselves and then to help others; to give and never have to receive." His words. My sisters and I have already accepted charity from Tsai Che, the official, in his household.[11] To be disgraced into further condolences is unbearable for any retention of our good name.

## Late Spring 1868

My good mother, if we had known, you could be living now. A wise man has told me of some drug that may have relieved your pain, but alas you have chosen not to be here. Today my heart is heavy that you are no longer with us. Uncle has relayed your words to me. Yes, I will have courage and present a good face to this world, and I will accept this fate. My learning will be put to use, but I can no longer remain here. Sadly, there is little money left and perhaps it is fated that I leave this village, leave my home.

*

Word has come telling me of my good mother's depraved burial. A sad burial, with no family land where she could rest, is of great disgrace. What is left but disgrace? The light

---

11  Tsai Che was a local official, and the diary here seems to suggest that Wong and his sisters may have sought refuge in Tsai's house.

fades early still, and I use the hours to meditate, to ponder about this burdening, toilsome world. The master's family returns soon. I must not allow myself to visit them too often, particularly the enjoyable children. Mourning disturbs children too much, they who are so full of living.

Some wise words from the honoured Tseng-Kuang: "Man cannot for a thousand days on end enjoy the good, just as the flower cannot bloom a hundred days." Thus my days of innocent good are forever lost. One day I will regain my open face, my happiness and peace, though now it must be accepted that the seventh year is one of hardship and toil.

## Autumn 1868

There is no hope of re-establishing any honour to our name nor any hope of having any land in this village. My sisters have, these past days, entered into their marriages in silence, with no feasting to welcome them. They were not even accepted into their original proposed positions. Lum Pei has made Second Sister his third concubine, though she maintains she is quite satisfied to remain in that house. As nameless women, they have no choice but to accept their given positions. I dare not chasten Lum Pei for his actions now that he is the head of his family. Second Sister is so beautiful – how I wish I could have afforded a carriage for her. To have to enter another's house in blue is surely a sorrowful omen. If only Lum Pei could have waited until these three years were over, Second Sister would have worn the red silks so well. However, at least they are well kept and my own stomach has been well attended. Such luxury to eat duck once again. I will never again take it for granted.

*

Master advises me that my progress in the readings is satis-factory, but the results of his appeal to the courts to hear my plea remain unknown. It will now be best to prepare to travel to the good Sai Ling's household, for, in that respect, I will have food until I am allowed to take the examinations. Once more I am indebted to the master for his aid.

*

I am leaving in several days for the coastal village of Sai Ling's very proper house. May I be able to add to his veneration.

# A GOOD FACE TO THIS WORLD

In the first few diary entries of 1867, Dukesang Wong writes about the loss of his father to murder, his mother to depression, and his good name to the vagaries of public sympathy. These entries reveal an educated young man with a facility for language, and though his emotions reflect his youth, he also displays a relative ease with expressing his feelings and internal conflicts. The crisis that his family faced during this period is at the forefront of these early entries, but the details that precipitated the crisis are missing. The diary excerpts chosen by Wong's granddaughter never explicitly explain the circumstances, nor do they describe the death of Wong's father, a magistrate, as murder. Thankfully, however, many of the story's details have been passed down as family history.

The Wong family story suggests that at a banquet held to celebrate the magistrate's ruling in a land dispute – a banquet hosted by the family who benefitted from that decision – a servant had been bribed by the competing family to poison the magistrate's food. The effect was immediate, but death came slowly. Dukesang Wong watched his father die over several hours. As he describes in his journal, he was horrified to see his father's fingernails turning black, a symptom of arsenic poisoning. Reading between the lines suggests that there may have been some element of corruption in the results of the original land dispute. Alternatively, the appearance of corruption might have led the aggrieved party to take such severe action. Whatever the facts, after the magistrate's death, many villagers turned against his family, and local officials stripped them of their properties and entitlements, suggesting that the magistrate, not the poisoner, was considered the disgraced and dishonoured party.

Wong writes about his father's "glorious banner," a symbol of standing in the community and a sign of advanced education, being torn from their house by the people of the village. Local officials were involved in the confiscation of the family home. Quarters were sectioned off for the women, and Wong was banished from the compound. Whether the local enmity was due to the particular circumstance of his father's decision in the land dispute is uncertain, but he asks, "How am I to show my face anywhere?"

He also writes of the conflict he felt around the expectation of vengeance. Feudal tradition demanded that a son seek revenge for the murder of his father, while his Confucian education taught a different path. It is Confucius who is most often cited for having written, "Before you embark on a journey of revenge, dig two graves." The conflicted young man writes in his diary that he despises "the duties required" by the vengeance tradition – yet he cannot despise the man who brought about the circumstances, meaning, most likely, the servant who poisoned the food.

Wong goes on to confess a fear that his teacher, the man he calls "the master," has been away from the village for three weeks due to the events surrounding his father's dishonour. Masters were private tutors hired by elites to prepare their sons for the bureaucratic administration of Imperial China. They often had very close relationships with their employing families. Wong's friend Chan is trying to contact the master, but Wong fears that despite his studying, his life's newly contentious circumstances may end his chances for the second-level degree. By early autumn he learns from another friend that a petition to restore his father's honour has been unsuccessful. The decision was made by the court in Peiping, an early colonial name for China's capital city Beijing. The humiliation Wong feels after the decision, will haunt him for years to come. More than twenty years after the magistrate's death, on a return visit he makes to China, Dukesang Wong will still be preoccupied with the restoration of his father's good name.

During these weeks in the autumn and early winter of 1867, Wong's mother increasingly suffers from what he refers to as her "anguished lunacy." She has unbound her feet as a sign of her utter despair. The painful and misogynist practice of foot binding, which often caused malformation and broken bones, had become common for the very young daughters of elite families. Among the mandarinate it was thought to improve the girls' marriage prospects. Both the binding and unbinding were extremely painful processes. Wong imagines that, were he allowed to see his mother, he might know how to talk to her and give her some relief. He is also worried that his uncle's attendance on his mother is inappropriate. This uncle was his father's younger brother, and Wong fears that the attention shown to his mother will be misread and add to their humiliation. He reveals a disturbing symptom of his mother's mental state when he writes, "she wills her own end." Wong also writes that his mother has advised him to leave the site of all their misery, their home village. However, he seems not to share her tainted opinion of his birthplace. According to his granddaughter, in diary entries not included in the translation, he only ever referred to this unnamed village as "sweet native land."

In the spring of 1868, a year after his father's death, Dukesang Wong adds a sad but not surprising entry to his diary. In a direct address to his mother, he tells of her death by suicide. Rather than go on living with the grief and shame of the past year, she has taken her own life. According to family history, she drowned after throwing herself into a well in the garden of their dispossessed home. In his address to his mother, Wong writes that had he known she was about to end her life, he could have acquired a drug that may have helped with the depression. In her notes accompanying the translation, his granddaughter suggests the drug was opium.

Most of what follows in this section is Wong's ongoing distress about both the dishonour of his mother's burial in a common graveyard and the unhappy circumstances of his sisters' marriages, all due to the loss of his family's good name. Second Sister became third wife in her marriage – more a concubine than a wife – and much to her brother's shame and regret, she wore the blue of mourning at her wedding rather than the red of brides. He is equally ashamed that his sister did not ride a carriage or a litter to her wedding, the normal conveyance for brides of the mandarin class. A few months later, unable to take the exams for his second degree without the court's approval, Wong accepts the position of tutor in the home of Sai Ling, a friend and colleague of Wong's master. In the late winter of 1869, two years after beginning his diaries, he leaves the unnamed village of his birth north of Beijing and travels to the house of Sai on the Bohai Sea near the city of Tianjin.

# THE OCEAN IS NOT AT PEACE

## Spring 1869

Life is stable again, at last. I am now settled. This house is very suitable for contemplation, and my allotted rooms are luxurious compared to my recent meagre quarters. The lands around this home slope to the sea, and the winds are now warming the slopes. The grass is already green. This entire place befits contemplation and a wiser pace of life.

I have acquired a servant who is quite pleasant-faced, from a very needy family, so the little beggar will do nearly anything well if instructed. I would like to teach him to read. Imagine having a literate servant. As yet I have not spoken to him of this, but I will tomorrow. May the souls of my parents understand. It seems pointless not to converse intelligently with his honourable family and allow their expressions of gratitude to pass for my helping their level of knowledge increase. Indeed, if they were not here, I should not be surviving so well.

*

My life until this point has become distant in my mind. I will never, however, forget the blackened fingers of my

father – they remain vivid in my mind. Fourth Uncle
has honoured me by visiting this village. He will stay for
some time in this area. Reassurance of my health, he says.
Though I wonder what other reasons there might be. Still,
I am happy to see him, even though his face reminds me
of my good mother. In this evening light, I see her painful
suffering before she left this earth. Enough now, as I must
contemplate my lessons.

Sai Ling, my intelligent student, is progressing well
and learning at a good pace. As befitting to a young girl I
suppose, she learns piously, but finds the great books very
difficult, and can only repeat what I instruct her. Her eyes
seem to want to know more, but she never questions me.
Asking her to question me is embarrassing for her ...

The ocean is not at peace. Daily the waves roar and
disturb my contemplation, drawing my attention away to
their movements. This location greatly disturbs me. It is,
however, part of existence, and I see eternity with all its
secrets unknown to me – but the roar constantly bothers
my soul, my inner peace.

## Summer 1872

Revered child of this great house, I dare not say to you in
words what I feel toward you. Once declared, the dishonour would be upon you as well as me. I could never show
my face again. It is not for me, now, to aspire to have you,
and you are already betrothed. My thoughts and feelings
of attachment for you will necessarily grow weaker as you
prepare for your life – for you must finally meet your true

master, and I will have been nothing more than a transient teacher. The stars missed in my life, but it is at least a life. Better, therefore, to carry it out.

*

My child, so very dear to my existence, I cannot ask you to meet me other than those few hours during your lessons. Concentration demands the pure mind and inner peace. Stillness and calmness is yet to be controlled in you. The freedom of your movement offends me. Do not tempt my control, as it is not in my position to seek you.

## Late Winter 1873

My journal, I should remove some pages from you upon reading my turmoil in words and thoughts last year. It might be best to retain them, however, to teach me emotional control. I have become wiser.

I am now in the benevolent employ of Sen Yutseng, as teacher to his oldest son. The young man will one day be truly wise. Amazingly enough, Sen seems pleased with my limited knowledge. He tells me how learned I am. Me, learned, not even possessing the second degree! One day I will have enough money to undertake the examination for that esteemed position. People have said that the venerable Kiang[12] will rule the courts. It is known he had great charity

---

12  Wong is probably referring to Chang Chih-tung, known today as Zhang Zhidong, a sometime reformer and one of the most highly regarded officials of the late Qing dynasty.

for my father's house. The joy in this thought now over-
whelms my daily thoughts.

## 1876

Today I met an Englishman who seems to be knowledgeable
and with whom I spent the entire afternoon. He tells me
of a Christ, a saviour, and that this Christ died for my soul.
It is an interesting concept: my soul to be saved – but from
what? There is no reason for this salvation. It appears to
be against the order of the life I know and have travelled
through so far in my limited years. The Englishman cannot
have any classical knowledge whatsoever, but he does seem
to be well versed in his philosophy.

*

My former village life seems to have faded from my
thoughts, even though the picture of my good father in
his death remains vividly imprinted on my mind. Our
name has been dishonoured forever, and it appears I can
do nothing to correct this terrible state of affairs. I cannot
destroy another person because they have been caught in
the middle of a feud and are being used as a tool to demonstrate the anger of an avenging family. Not only is taking a
life a useless act, but such an act will mean that our family
will cease to exist, even in this dishonoured state. No one
will be able to carry on the traditions of our name, nor
ensure that our ancestors live onward through the souls of
the generations to come. It is my duty to remain alive, yet
also my duty to correct the dishonour to our name. All I am

now is a low-faced man. But at least I have not dishonoured any other family, even though teaching the young boy is becoming extremely difficult. Sen is always gentle and kind to his son and acts more like a woman toward him, showing great weakness toward the boy's demands. The boy is very intelligent, however, and I will gladly impart all the knowledge I possess to him.

I have met with the Englishman on four more occasions. He is not English at all but French – but in any case, also a barbaric land I am told. They have a great deal of violence and many rebellions against their rulers and elders and even against one another of the same position. This man, however, seems at peace with himself, accepting himself and his position, even though somehow he cannot accept this world. Rather, he rejects it for a better world, one to which he will go after his death. Perhaps it is his way of denying the turmoil and continual disagreement from which he comes. His ancestors must be highly esteemed and venerable in their land for him to want to join them rather than having children to perpetuate their spirits. He is indeed a curious yet earnest person.

He believes he will join his ancestors in the eternity of spirit. He also thinks highly of Christ, a suffering man put to death by his own people for teaching a way of goodness in life. He was a revolutionary for his time, yet his people did not listen to his ideas and killed him. Such a violent act! His ideas should have been heard and discussed. My own thoughts are certainly against the idea of the afterlife this white man speaks about, yet I have a great desire to question him much more. Today he told me of the mother-virgin of the man Christ. Perhaps the order of life here is so wrong and misarranged for him that in his poor mind he thinks it lunacy – although the peasants always have many various magical happenings in their beliefs and conceptions, too. It is all a strange and curious philosophy.

## Early Spring 1879

Today I may have dishonoured my great teacher in accepting another philosophy from a foreign land. Christian teachings are, however, just another point of view toward this life in which we all must exist, and it is certain, I think, that these lessons are about a good life of giving and helping other people. Knowledge must encompass all, including foreign teachings. I can only accept the lessons, however, as wisdom and knowledge. This other idea of the Frenchman, that Christ believed he was put to death to save the spirits of all humankind, I cannot accept. It is beyond my powers of understanding. The sages have written of a great guide and teacher, born of a meeting of stars, and therefore it is reasonable that his Christ may be that same teacher. There have been records of several other such occurrences with great teachers arising shortly after such meetings of the stars. My own life is humble and bearable, and now there is even some order and stability. But the real peace of the inner spirit eludes me still, as it surely will until I am truly fulfilled. Yet the Frenchman is as alone as I am, but he has an inner peace. It is in his eyes, while I am always striving to attain it.

The Frenchman wishes that I accept the fact of the short length of our lives, and of the limitations on what we can do with that life. He suggests preparing for the life that follows the death of the body. I cannot accept that, cannot contemplate such acceptance of a life of the spirit after death. Our sages have all taught us of the order of life as it flows. The Frenchman's belief in a beautiful afterlife is completely against the great order by which we have lived so long.

The Frenchman's professed philosophy also includes the concept of one wife and woman at a time for all of a man's lifetime. This is interesting, as they would offer their total devotion to one woman for life, yet their marriages, like ours, are arranged between their houses. It is difficult to understand even in terms of numbers of females to males, so I ask myself how one reconciles only one woman when the order of life demands that all women must exist with men. Our order sets forth the better way, I think.

## Late Spring 1879

This is a memorable day in my life! Yin-ling has promised his youngest daughter to me for a second wife – should I have sufficient fortune to maintain her. She is an interesting and wanted child and came into my sight for a few moments while searching for her esteemed father's younger sister. I wish to see more of her and watch her grow into womanhood. The agreement has been made, however, and I must abide until she has become a woman.

## Spring 1880

I have decided to venture to that country they call "the Land of the Golden Mountains." The next ship that departs for those shores is the one which I shall be on. Because I cannot build upon my own land in this country, it is right that I should attempt to seek land over the ocean. Several men with whom I have talked tell me of the opportunities of establishing a home over in those western lands. While Lin is still yet growing, I can afford the time now to build a real home to call mine. Perhaps it will prove to be too strange and foreign a land to which to adapt myself and bring Lin, but I must try it and have experience of it in the event that it is a better land that will allow me to once again establish a real home. The voyage is not too costly, and Sen's young boy is maturing into manhood, needing a much more knowledgeable teacher than I can be, though it is best that I retain my fees until the time of departure. Tomorrow I will finalize the necessary arrangements.

## Late Summer 1880

I will be going today, embarking on the voyage to America. My destination is the Big City where, I am told, there are several other Chinese families. Perhaps they are also knowledgeable about my own village and the area, so that I shall not be alone. Chan told me earlier today that he is contemplating also coming to America soon. I wish he would come with me now, for adventures such as this are foreign and new to me, and my soul's order is awry and upset.

The ship we are taking is a Christian missionary vessel and is very small for such a large ocean, so many of us will have to learn to sway with its movements. I am also told that there is a substantial amount of Oriental gold and true jade on this ship, destined for the markets of France and England. I feel sorrowful that such goods are being taken from their homeland instead of remaining with this country for the appreciation of generations to come. White people surely cannot value jade as we do: it has little meaning for them except as a colourful adornment, and then only on the women. I fear the beauty of the intricate craftsmanship fashioned out of stone will become very lost in those foreign lands.

It has been said that the land to which I am now heading is wild and uncivilized, and that people kill each other daily. All the business and the laws are controlled by white people, while we are not permitted to rule over our own actions. There surely must be some areas where it is not so barbaric: my life doesn't yet have the signs of impending death, and my family has not yet carried on its name. With no wife and children, my life has still to be lived, and I am curious what this new land will bring.

*

I am heavy-hearted to say farewell to this land of my soul, my father. There have been many moments of joy and peace for me here, even though my recent past years have been difficult and somewhat shameful. It saddens me that I can no longer say I have a home village here, though the course of this life dictates that I must leave.

*

The group of people on the ship is surely not honourable. Daily they wail about the bad conditions and forget that the squalor on our level will not be eternal. Land will be so stable and will feel so good after the time on this ship: this is a good thought. I am happy that the good physician has given us a stabilizing broth to drink, for the rough seas are truly hard to bear. It has helped many of the weaker ones escape their suffering. There are many people of the working peasantry on this ship. They burn incense to their ancestors, and the smell is stifling in this humidity, though I thank the humidity, for at least the fires will not consume the creaking boards of the ship. In the evening when the seas become calm, the poor labourers sit on the deck and sing, expressing more of their sorrows in their untrained, wailing voices. They express their emotions so much: it is most shameful for them and for me to hear them. It is not for me to speak to them, however; their pains are most difficult for them to bear. The priests try to teach them prayers, but the language is foreign and the ideas fall upon deaf ears, while my translation attempts in our language feel strange even to my own ears.

# THE ORDER OF LIFE AS IT FLOWS

Dukesang Wong was twenty-three when he took up his position as tutor in the house of Sai. His first impressions suggest a sense of great relief after the turmoil of his recent life. An intelligent young man, he is admired by his employer and satisfied with the progress of Sai Ling, his young female student. While it wasn't common for girls to receive classical educations, it wasn't unknown. From what can be gleaned from the diary, Sai Ling was a free-spirited and favoured child, and Wong finds her to be intelligent, pious, and demure. Wong also acquired a servant, a young man from a needy family. He imagines teaching the boy to read, and though it was clearly a servant–master relationship, Wong's interest in educating him may suggest a somewhat more enlightened view than might otherwise have been expected from the mandarin class.

The final entry for 1869 hints that not all is rosy in the house of Sai. Wong has begun to feel disturbed by the ocean and the distracting roar of the waves. It is at this moment that the first significant gap in the diaries occurs, a gap of three years from 1869 to 1872. We are left with no explanation for his distracted state until the diary resumes in the summer of 1872. But in the first entry of that year it quickly becomes clear that during the time Wong stayed in the house of Sai he fell in love with his student, and here he uses the safety of his diary to express his real feelings for Sai Ling.

As the tutor grew more and more attracted to his young student, his concern and anxiety about the attraction also grew. Like most of the young women of the period in China, Sai Ling had been betrothed in an arranged marriage. Wong was acutely aware of the inappropriateness of his attraction. Also seeing himself as nothing more than a lowly "transient" teacher, he felt unworthy of her. Nevertheless, the language of his entries in 1872 conveys a deep and sometimes consuming love for Sai Ling. It wasn't surprising that the seaside home that began as "suitable for contemplation," became the place where the roar of waves disturbed his "inner peace."

The journal picks up again six months later in the winter of 1873. Wong has left the Sai family and taken new employment in the home of the warlord Sen Yutseng, as tutor to his eldest son. The entry begins with Wong contemplating removing several pages of his notebook. At some later date he did remove the pages, which explains some of the missing three years. But it also leaves a large gap in the story of the house of Sai and the events that led to Wong's departure, including any details concerning the relationship with Sai Ling and its implications.

The location of his new tutoring position is unknown, but Wong's granddaughter speculates that the move may have required him to travel farther south, possibly as far as Shanghai. He made a few acquaintances in his new community, including a man he first believed to be an English missionary – and later discovered to be French. The Treaty of Nanjing in 1842 opened Chinese cities to European concessions and the Shanghai French Concession was established in 1849. French Jesuit missionaries set up the first Catholic school there that same year. An alternative possibility would have Wong remaining in the area around Tianjin where the Jesuits also had a historic presence in the French Concession there. The Jesuit philosopher and scholar Pierre Teilhard de Chardin made his home in the city a few years later. In this diary section Wong mentions Chan, his friend from his youthful days in the home village. Ongoing relationships with friends from those days would more likely have been maintained from the much closer city of Tianjin than from Shanghai.

Active missionaries in both coastal Chinese cities spoke Mandarin, while those in the southern provinces would have learned Cantonese. Wong and his missionary friend met several times for philosophical conversations and friendly debate, and it appeared not to matter to him whether the man was English or French since Wong judged most countries of the western world to be barbaric, always embroiled in foreign and civil wars or revolutions. In the early pages of his diaries, however, he seems to have very little concern for the many rebellions and wars in his own country.

In the course of his many conversations with the missionary, Wong became intrigued with the philosophies and teachings of Christianity. His diary becomes a dialogue between the tenets of Christianity and his own Confucian beliefs and cultural traditions. He suggests, with deference to his master, that there is much to admire philosophically about Christian beliefs, again revealing a willingness to at least examine new ideas. He also envies the inner peace of the missionary, a peace he believes he himself will not have until he is "truly fulfilled," meaning, according to his granddaughter, until he is in a consummated marriage at the head of a family.

Nevertheless, he firmly defends the Chinese beliefs and traditions he has grown up with, comparing them favourably with the Christian beliefs he finds farfetched and uninformed. Wong finds, for example, the Christian idea that a man should be devoted to one woman to be inferior to the Chinese tradition of multiple wives and concubines. Given the number of pages he devotes to conversations with the missionary, it seems he took great pleasure in philosophical debate.

By comparison, in all the excerpts from the years he was employed in the home of Sen Yutseng, he says little about his life there with the family, other than to suggest he has imparted all the knowledge he can to the sons. He does, however, continue to write about the dishonour his own family has borne, always imagining the day when the courts will restore their good name.

Toward the end of this section we learn that Wong has become betrothed to Lin, the youngest daughter of a man called Yin-ling. Nothing more is said to identify the family. It is this piece of information, along with the dates which accompany the news, that causes the first confusion in the unfolding story of Dukesang Wong's life. In the translation, the diary report of the betrothal is dated between 1879 and 1880. But, according to a headstone in a Vancouver cemetery, Lin, the child described in this diary entry who grew up to become Dukesang Wong's wife of more than thirty-five years, was born in 1880.

It is possible that Wong recorded the date of the betrothal incorrectly, but the dates of following events appear accurate. A more likely explanation for the proximity of Lin's birthdate and betrothal date is the not entirely uncommon practice in Imperial China for infant girls to be promised and even given in marriage. The children were called "little brides," and in some cases, these infant betrothals were financial transactions. It is possible that Yin-ling promised Lin to Wong and money changed hands. Wong writes that Lin was promised to him as a second wife, probably because it was expected that he would marry a first wife long before Lin came of age. Wong was thirty-five years older than Lin; in the patriarchal structure of Imperial China, that was not unusual. And just as arranged marriages were traditional, so was polygamy.

In some of these "little bride" marriages, the child was given to the family of the future groom to raise as their own until she came of age. While that doesn't appear to be the case here, we do know that Lin was raised by guardians, and that they emigrated to Canada to be near her future husband a year before she reached marriageable age. As Wong's granddaughter explained, these personal questions were never discussed by her family, and clarity may now be impossible. Nevertheless, the questions will return with later entries.

In the final entry of this section, Wong reveals another surprising decision. With no previous indication that a declaration like this was coming, he announces he will leave China and travel to America, following in the footsteps of thousands who preceded him. It was a land he imagined full of possibilities no longer available to him in China. In this "Land of the Golden Mountains," he hopes to establish a home for himself and his betrothed; he also holds to the hope that a new beginning might restore honour to his name.

Wong boarded a ship in the summer of 1880 and set sail for Gold Mountain. He believed he was bound for San Francisco, which he called "the Big City." He doesn't identify the port of departure, nor does he give particulars of the ship, except to say that it was a "very small Christian missionary vessel." In describing the conditions on board, he is grateful for the dampness, "for at least the fires will not consume the creaking boards," a phrase which seems to suggest a wooden sailing ship, although steamships were also being used at the time. He describes a rough crossing and when he talks about "our level," he is most likely referring to steerage, the cargo hold on most ships. During these periods of mass migration, the holds were often turned into communal living quarters with rows of sleeping platforms and overcrowded conditions.

He also expresses concern that the ship carries "true jade" destined for overseas markets. Throughout the period, collectors in North America and Europe were seeking carved pieces in significant numbers.

Confucius had described jade as the stone of truth and wisdom, and Wong believed its cultural significance for the Chinese was neither understood nor shared by western collectors. It wasn't unusual for jade to be transported on missionary ships, since many missionaries were themselves collectors. Pieces "collected" by European and North American missionaries in the nineteenth century can be seen today in the collections of several museums, including the Metropolitan Museum of Art in New York City, Toronto's Royal Ontario Museum, and the British Museum in London. Of course jade wasn't the only treasure taken from China to the west. Ceramics and ancient scrolls and other priceless artifacts were plundered throughout the nineteenth century. The Centre for Art Law in New York reported in July, 2019, that "over 1.6 million looted Chinese antiquities reside in museums across the world."[13]

Wong reveals a variety of emotions about leaving China, including sadness for the loss of his birthplace and his childhood. He also expresses anxiety about the unknown place to which he is travelling, a place where laws and business are conducted for white people by white people. He even acknowledges some fear about his personal safety in the "barbaric" lands "where people kill each other daily." We can imagine that stories were circulating in the port and on board ship about lawless gunslinging in the "Wild West."

On the high seas, Wong conveys frustration with his fellow travellers, in particular with the public emotions of the "people of the working peasantry." His perspective offers glimpses of the privilege inherent in his upbringing, a privilege that will fade upon his arrival in Gold Mountain, when he realizes the extent of the racism there – and of the struggles he and his companions will face together, regardless of their background.

---

13    For decades the Chinese have been asking for the return of the plunder that was carried out of the country throughout the nineteenth century. There are even stories of the Chinese government hiring thieves to steal back artifacts from western museums that refuse to return them. A few of the items known to have been stolen have turned up in Chinese museums.

"Chinese immigrants on the deck of the 'Black Diamond' (sailing vessel, BC)," circa 1889, by Robert W. Refort. LIBRARY AND ARCHIVES CANADA/ROBERT WILSON REFORD AND FAMILY FONDS/A118185.

"Chinese at work on C.P.R. (Canadian Pacific Railway) in Mountains," 1884, by Ernest Brown. LIBRARY AND ARCHIVES CANADA/ERNEST BROWN COLLECTION/C006686.

Paddlewheeler at Yale, 1882, photographer unknown. IMAGE HP009730
COURTESY OF THE ROYAL BC MUSEUM AND ARCHIVES.

Chinese workers on the CPR. ORIGINAL SOURCE AND PHOTOGRAPHER
UNKNOWN.

"Chinese camp (Canadian Pacific Railway), Kamloops, British
Columbia," 1886, by Edouard Deville. LIBRARY AND ARCHIVES CANADA/
WILLIAM MOLSON MACPHERSON FONDS/C021983.

"Chinese work gang, Canadian Pacific Railway tracks near summit, British Columbia," 1889 (NA-3740-29), by William Notman and Son.
COURTESY OF GLENBOW ARCHIVES, ARCHIVES AND SPECIAL COLLECTIONS, UNIVERSITY OF CALGARY. IMAGED CROPPED.

A Chinese workers' camp of log bunkhouses at Keefers, near Lytton, photographer unknown. IMAGE I-30869 COURTESY OF THE ROYAL BC MUSEUM AND ARCHIVES.

This much-reproduced image shows a group of Chinese railway workers, photographer unknown. IMAGE D-07548 COURTESY OF THE ROYAL BC MUSEUM AND ARCHIVES.

A view of New Westminster in the 1890s, looking east, showing the city's Chinatown. Ying Tai and Co., on the corner of Carnarvon Street and Tenth Street, can be seen in the upper right quadrant. Photographer unknown. NEW WESTMINSTER ARCHIVE, IHP4313.

"Chinese Street, Victoria, BC," 1886, by C. Deville. LIBRARY AND ARCHIVES CANADA/NATURAL RESOURCES CANADA FONDS/A053604.

The gravestone of Dukesang Wong and his son, Harry Wong, at Mountain View Cemetery in Vancouver, BC. Photo by Wayne Worden. COURTESY OF MOUNTAIN VIEW CEMETERY.

The gravestone of Lin Ying, Dukesang Wong's wife, and their daughter, Elsie Hoe, mother of Wanda Joy Hoe, who translated her grandfather's diaries. Photo by Wayne Worden. COURTESY OF MOUNTAIN VIEW CEMETERY.

# The Gold Mountain Diary

# THESE LANDS ARE WILD

## Portland, Oregon, USA

**Late Summer 1880**

For over three weeks we have been docked in the harbour
of this new land, but we have not been able to set our feet
upon the land. The authorities have said we may have
diseases and must remain here in the ship. We, who hold
cleanliness so high and propriety so dear, to have the kinds
of diseases that those white authorities say – it is totally
unworthy of them. Left here in the squalor of this deck as
if we are animals, even less than dogs! It is ironic that those
white authorities keep us here to prevent disease, while
we all wish to set our feet upon land and clean ourselves. I
really wonder at their reasoning.

*

We have at last set our feet upon land. I am pleased to see
happier faces on my ship companions as they excitedly
scurry around to establish themselves. Portland is a good
place, even though we hear of tales of wild and crazy events
outside town. I doubt the truth of these tales.

## Late Winter 1881

It has been some time since I have had any desire to write
in this journal. The misery I see daily disturbs my thoughts,
and I find it very difficult to think clearly about anything
except my companions' suffering in this new land to which
we all so desired to come. There is so little work to be
obtained near our dwellings, and our meagre foodstuffs are
hard to replenish, even from the other ships which come
from our homeland. Fortunately, we have our own companionship, and there is enough wood to burn in this frozen
land. The rivers are not safe to fish through the ice, as the
ice cannot hold even such little men as we. Several people
have drowned, and we cannot bury them now, not even in
this foreign land. We will soon need to obtain work and find
our own land away from this town, to escape the degrading
treatment of the white people in the town.

## Early Summer 1881

I have at last been promised a position laying railway under
the employment of a white man further north of this town
in a place called the "Saltwater City." The work in this town
mostly consists of service, in attendance to families here. To
work in such a manner is certainly not a great honour, as
I daily see servants being extremely ill-treated and beaten
by their masters. This new work that I will be doing is good
labour, paying in gold, and I will have some hours for my
own living and contemplation. Again, I am indebted to
Lo-en-lai for his great aid in obtaining this work, but I hope

to repay him someday soon. I do not want to indebt myself continuously to strangers, but rather become a worthy man of my own. I must save as much as I am able and live humbly in piety, as my goals must be reached, yet I am continuously becoming indebted to others for their help and cannot repay them in the correct manner of my position here. My years of learning, however, will be a great aid, and I shall try to teach once I have saved some money. Chen's family already has need of guiding in this manner, and he is able to afford such a teacher for his son, though what that child lacks most is the guidance of his mother and relatives.

These lands are wild! Only this evening I witnessed a man being violently beaten by another of his own kind. I could not believe what my eyes were seeing. There were white people standing around, and not one of them moved to stop the beater. Surely there are no manners and rules here. The waste and senselessness is hard to look upon. Our people would talk through differences and hear each other, no matter how grave the problem, but those white people fight and die in disorganized combat. Such is their law and order, such is their barbaric justice. A man near me said that it was their way and only fair, the honour code of their traditions, to thus settle their differences. It is like the tales of the sages, when settling of differences was done in ancient China by survival of physical strength and not by an arbitrator.

# A LAND ALREADY FULL OF SADNESS

## New Westminster, British Columbia

### Autumn 1881

It is hard, this labouring, but my body seems to be strong enough. The people working with me are good, strong men. There are many of us working here, but the laying of the railroad progresses very slowly. It seems we move two stones a day! And they want this railway built across these high mountains, some two thousand miles! Even over the plains of our homeland, such railways took over a generation to build, so I can imagine these white people will face failed dreams.

I've heard there is a need for working men in another city across the water, in loading ships and cutting lumber, but those foreign people will not treat us well. They constantly examine our dwellings, calling them filthy, and in that city they treat our people worse than here, some have said like dogs.

\*

I have been honoured today. The Chinese workers have elected me as their spokesman with the contractor, to speak of our good deeds. I am truly surprised that the workers did not choose Chen,[14] since he is more proficient in English. I can speak much better in the learned language of our people, but English is hard to speak. However, I must try to obtain better medicine and food for us to eat. We won't be strong if we do not have enough food in our stomachs.

## Spring 1882

Many Chinese people are here now, working on this railway. Some are from the Big City and many others are from Kwangchow and the Canton area,[15] speaking in their village language. It is a little difficult to be a spokesman for them, as their language is hard to understand, and they aren't able to write. Chen has returned to his home village. I miss his company, and I would also like to return to our homeland.

*

Yesterday, I returned from Victoria. It is a beautiful and clean city compared to this town in the mountains. I became known to the Indians here during the trip, and their help in the return journey was great. They are solitary people, but they know the land so well. My experience is so

---

14 Chen and Wong became friends while working together on the railway, but Chen returned to China within a year.

15 I assume that here Wong is referring both to the city and the region, using "Canton area" to include the Siyi and the Pearl River Delta.

limited in those small boats in which it is so hard to travel. How I wished to have a horse to ride!

I despair at being able to save so little these days, but the small garden Chen left in my care has been helping my food supply. How good the fresh green vegetables taste. If only it was warm enough, I could become truly well by eating fresh food.

## Early Autumn 1883

My soul cries out. I wish I had never experienced such bad days as those in which we now live. Many of our people have been so very ill for such a long time, and there has been no medicine nor good food to give them. Even the strongest of us are weak without medicine to fight against these diseases, which spread very rapidly. It is such a sorrowful sight. The white doctor has told us the illnesses come from lack of fresh food, but we cannot grow any fresh food, as all of us, including the white people, are moving constantly with the work we have to do. The good doctor has gone to the larger town in search of better food for the very ill, but I am afraid that the medicines will not arrive here to these poor gutter-shelters. I would have liked to accompany him, but my body does not have the strength or desire.

These are troubled times for us Chinese. There has been word among the employing company that we are not good workers and do not work enough for the schedules and plans of the railway owners. How does anyone work when so ill? Many are killed when such words are spoken, and we are becoming more like dogs biting at one another. My meagre attempts at talking about being humble and waiting for better days are senseless. My words mean less than nothing. I am of so little help to everyone.

*

The frost has fallen early and only the bok choy survives in my boxes. I wonder when I shall have laboured enough to journey back to my home village. Perhaps I will not ever be able to return, but how I long for those childhood days. Chen has sent words that tell of turmoil in China, but he does not say where.

## 1885

I am truly alone amid the dying. The leaders of the white people demand money – our poor savings – taken from we who have so little, given to those who are not so taxed. Some who are very ill have taken to spending their days in the opium shacks, with little food and even less strength. This is a bad omen.

*

At last the frost has left and the grass grows on the hills. The life around my shelter is starting again, and my soul feels much less burdened. We have been burying some of the people who died over the hard, foodless days, but the sight of those dead is hard. Wing Sun's savings were not enough even to send his body to the Saltwater City, and I walked to his grave today to apologize. Wan Chu derided me for bowing, but it is in our traditions and manner to do so. The dead are higher in station than we who remain on this earth. Wan said we must follow the ways of the white people, so that we are not considered separate and strange by them. But they bury their dead so casually and never show signs of remembrance or honour. The dead once lived among us and also moulded our lives, making it imperative that we honour them as we carry them with us.

*

There is much work to be done and not enough people to labour at it. So many of us Chinese suffered and died recently; I cannot recount them all. But the western people will not allow us to land here any longer, while they scold us for not working enough. How these acts wear my soul down to nothing. Kwong tells us about the laws the white people have enacted to prohibit any further landing of our people. I cannot understand why. The work is great, and there aren't enough labourers. The Indians are not working these days, and the Hindu people cannot labour as we are able to. But my words are meaningless, and my strength to speak now falls upon deaf ears and closed eyes. These mighty lands are great to gaze upon, but the laws made here are so small.

## Spring 1886

For many days now I have been so tired that I could not continue to write in this journal. Master Dufferin[16] has been driving us to finish the tracks of the railway, and my

---

16   Clearly not a reference to Lord Dufferin, the Governor General.

depleted body seems like it will forego this life. Dufferin is a real taskmaster, but he has also been a generous person at times. Perhaps someday I will be able to aid our people as he does. He's been helping my young neighbour with her tasks and the heavy load she bears, and he greatly concerns himself with her safety. The others have gossiped that he must take his pleasure from her, but when I have seen her, her eyes are not those of a woman but of a young girl. I have seen Dufferin bolt her door for her, so how then could he be so inappropriate?

I am told that there are three men of my village over here in the Land of the Golden Mountains. They are said to be in a settlement north of this town. Perhaps I'll soon be able to visit their settlement and talk with them about our home village. It has been a very long time since I have heard any words spoken in my own language and about the news of my homeland.

## Summer 1886

Work has brought us back to the Saltwater City. There is some fresh food for us and enough fish to fill our stomachs. So many have suffered from diseases and have been working their skin off, appearing more like skeletons, so sick without food and rest. Even the fresh food here will have little effect on some of the poor frail bodies, but all of us are greatly relieved.

We share our dwellings now with three others who have come from a town that recently burned down. Such sorrowful sights they are, and they seem to grovel at everything and think us wealthy. Their mannerisms disturb me a great deal, as they give such exaggerated deference to us and bow continuously, at every turn.

Times for us now are definitely changing, and the fortunes of our people need great care and guarding. There is so little we can do to change the way the white people see us, yet I do wish the weight of taxes on us was gone. One good event took place a few days ago, however – tea! Loads of tea for sipping. My young neighbour has prepared a feast for us to accompany the tea, and we all delight in these days.

*

Today, as it is a feast day in the western calendar, all the labourers are free to follow their own will. I decided to wander in the hills of this land. There are few books to read, and my own are too well read to interest me in any new way, so I will compose a few words about my own thoughts and ideas. I have pondered this fresh new land, yet it is a land already full of sadness. The people are beginning to pursue a search for gold. They say it glitters everywhere, and men die for it. It is a peculiar set of values, strange to my humble limited experience, where men fight one another for it. The masters have said, "Only ill will come from desiring material things one cannot obtain; only good will come from desiring good." I desire material things sufficient for my living, and to bring Lin to an established house. The glitter of gold will not bring her to me. It would be only too easily robbed from me, so I labour onward, being called foolish by some people. Is it a fool's dream to want to establish myself, to be well respected and a full man? In my home village, if people could see what goes on here, they would surely despise the violence there and leave the village for the invaders to conquer.

Today, Hsin Wun Ming resisted a young white man's attempt to rob him of his mother's newest jade piece, a beautiful stone. Hsin Wun Ming resorted to hitting the thief. When the young robber awoke, it amused us all how he stared at us in response to the offer of some chicken congee. The white man is always afraid of our food. The young devil rushed away as if we were offering him poison – although he should accept poison for the disgrace of being captured in his terrible act. It was laughable to see him scurry away, but I also felt a strange awe of this land, that such occurrences happen without any feeling of obligation to restore or correct them.

## Early Winter 1886

In my meditation last evening, I formed a decision. I will work here in this town, doing tailoring, in order to establish a house and have a good name among the Chinese here. Tailoring is a worthwhile trade that I can perform, and it will also help people who cannot purchase clothing from western tailors. There is not enough ready-made clothing from China, and there are no tailors to cut the cloth in our manner. I will be able to earn some money, enough to bring Lin over to this land. I am afraid for her life in our homeland, since all her family perished and she has no place to go. She is yet so young, although her letter has wisdom within it.[17] She has done well studying the books of the Sage, and her wisdom will be a great aid to me. I can just see myself, my disgraced self, in the eyes of the court and her guardian, having little to show and no degree band to wear. Yet Lin has been promised to me as my second wife. Ironic that I do not have a first, unless those brief moments with Su-Lin were first.

I must destroy this line of thought. It is not correct to be so flippant.

## Late Summer 1887

The coastal regions were certainly cooler than this place. The land is very dry, and dust continually cakes onto our skin as we work. Today I had to be treated by the town physician for exhaustion in my lungs. I need to rest, but I have yet to obtain enough funds to return to the Saltwater City to build a place to start tailoring. I thought that my strength was built up sufficiently in the south, but this land is far harsher and demands more strength than I have. I have been here for seven months and have only been doing labour on the railway. Mining coal brings more money, but the owners of the mines will no longer allow us poor people to work for them. There are no Chinese families here who I could teach, although the white people have schools for their children. I am very interested in their teachings and

---

17  Lin is six or seven years old at this time and in the care of guardians. They have probably schooled her to a limited extent in the Confucian tradition and helped her write a letter to Wong.

wish I could understand enough of their language to listen to their lessons.

My old way of life – my soul desires it, and my mind continually wanders to those days of no cares and worries. My dear father, if only you can see me now, labouring, using my physical strength to earn some food and hoarding the money paid to me!

*

My stars are well positioned! But the poor people who died in such a burial ground, so deep in the earth. People have said that hundreds perished as the walls of those dark caves crumbled. So many lives gone for such a meagre cause! Those peoples' families will surely face a hard winter, without any source of help with their losses.

## Late Autumn 1887

At last a ship full of our people's goods has arrived bringing such joy! We have teas and rice. We have spices and dried food. We will have a full year's celebration with such fortune!

## THE LAWS MADE HERE ARE SO SMALL

Despite Wong's belief that the ship he boarded was headed for San Francisco, it docked instead at Portland, Oregon. To his dismay, the Chinese passengers were held in quarantine in the ship's hold, sitting idly in the Portland harbour for three weeks. As he does often when laws seem to justify mistreatment, Wong challenges their illogic. Once the men are released, however, there is a period of optimism in his writing. Unfortunately it does not last long. Within a couple of months, the lack of work and the racism in Portland has a sobering impact, so much so that Wong is not able to bring himself to write anything for several weeks. Only the companionship and camaraderie of his countrymen keep him going. In describing the misery of these months in Portland, Wong once again reveals a growing humanist inclination that continues through much of the rest of his diaries.

When, in the early summer of 1881, Wong writes that he has "been promised a position" on a railway crew somewhere north of Portland, he initially seems to neither know nor care that the Land of the Golden Mountains is comprised of two separate countries, and that his new employment will take him from the United States to Canada. He writes that he is going to a place he calls the "Saltwater City," the only name he knew at that time for the city of New Westminster.[18] It was the first capital of the Colony of British Columbia – and, by 1881, the largest city on the provincial mainland.[19] For the first time in a while, Wong's

---

18  Wanda Joy was adamant that her grandfather referred to 1880–1885 New Westminster as "Saltwater City."
19  See Statistics Canada, "Canada Year Book 1895," www66.statcan.gc.ca /eng/1895-eng.htm.

optimism reappears as he imagines the independence this new contract could bring him.

This new sense of purpose leaves him imagining that he could be debt-free, a "worthy man," even a teacher. He favourably compares the "good labour" he will do building a railway with the demeaning house-servant jobs available in Portland, where he has seen Chinese servants "ill treated and beaten."

Wong's final diary entry before leaving for Canada describes a fight between two men in the street. He claims not to understand this act of violence, and is told it is the way disagreements are resolved in America. His response, "these lands are wild!," seems intended as a comparison to his homeland. Perhaps he misses the irony of the comparison. It is true that he didn't directly experience the wars and rebellions which dominated so much of China's history in the nineteenth century. But he did experience the violence of his own father's death. For him, though, that violence is not comparable to the gunslinger culture of his new home.


During the summer of 1881, Wong travelled north to Canada from Portland. In the translated excerpts, there is no mention of how he made the trip, but in the family's version of the story, he walked to Canada. His destination, the city of New Westminster, near the mouth of the Fraser River on Canada's Pacific Coast, had been the first capital of the colony of British Columbia from 1859 to 1866, when Victoria became the capital. While Dukesang Wong referred to New Westminster as the Saltwater City, others called it "Yi Fao," meaning "second port," to distinguish it from Victoria. With a population of 1,500 in 1881, the city was second in size only to Victoria on Vancouver Island. Both cities were commercial hubs, and both had agents working for the Canadian Pacific Railway, the company created to build the country's transcontinental rail line. Almost twenty kilometres northwest of New Westminster was a sparsely populated settlement called Granville. When it was chosen as the terminus for the newly completed CPR in 1886, the settlement changed its name to Vancouver. As it grew to exceed the population and importance of New Westminster, the Chinese community began to refer to Vancouver as the Saltwater City.

The Canadian federal government had promised the completion of the CPR to convince British Columbians to join Canada; the confederation had been born fourteen years earlier, in 1867, the same year

Magistrate Wong was poisoned. By 1881, work had begun on the most difficult section of the railway's route – precarious track beds cut from steep cliffs and tunnels blasted through mountainsides rising above the treacherous rapids of Fraser Canyon. Andrew Onderdonk, the American contractor charged with constructing that most difficult section, argued that the work could not be accomplished without the use of Chinese labour. Onderdonk told the then Prime Minister of Canada, Sir John A. Macdonald, that if workers were not brought from China, the project would probably not be completed. In this sentiment, he echoed former Governor of California and Central Pacific Railroad president Leland Stanford, who years before had wired U.S. President Andrew Johnson to say that "without [the Chinese workers] it would be impossible to complete the western portion of this great national enterprise within the time required by the Acts of Congress."[20] Of course, neither Onderdonk nor Stanford mentioned how much their own profits would grow by exploiting Chinese workers. When the government and people of British Columbia expressed their opposition to Onderdonk's plan to hire Chinese labourers, Prime Minister Macdonald told them they had a simple choice: they could have the railway, built in part by Chinese workers, or have no railway at all.

Part of Onderdonk's rationale for employing Chinese workers may well have been a labour shortage and an effort to lower costs, but another part was almost certainly his knowledge of the skills and character that Chinese labourers had earlier brought to their work prospecting for gold and building the Central Pacific Railroad across the American West. He knew they could lay a mile of track faster than Europeans and that their financial desperation led them to accept the most difficult and dangerous jobs. He knew they could strike a camp and move on to a new location in a matter of hours. And most importantly for Macdonald and for Onderdonk, because Chinese workers would be paid only half the wages of white workers, they would save the government millions and substantially increase the profits of the contractor and his backers. And so it was agreed. Chinese workers were brought north from San

---

20 United States Department of the Interior, *Report of the Secretary of the Interior,* in *Message of the President of the United States and Accompanying Documents to the Two Houses of Congress at the Commencement of the First Session of the Thirty-Ninth Congress* (Washington, DC: U.S. Government Printing Office, 1865), 990.

Francisco and the American northwest. And agents in Hong Kong were contracted to sign up workers in China and send them overseas.

The worst excesses of industrial capitalism were firmly embedded in the economies and social structures of the continent during this period, which came to be known as the Gilded Age. Though the American Civil War had resulted in the emancipation of the enslaved Black population of the United States just fifteen years earlier, the often cruel exploitation of workers, especially immigrant workers, continued in both the United States and Canada. Employers preyed on desperate men and women from countries as far-flung as China, Ireland, and India, paying starvation wages and exacerbating the anger and fear of the white North American working class. For the captains of industry, it was convenient to have that anger and fear directed at immigrant workers rather than at them. The Chinese and most other people of colour bore the brunt of growing racism and anti-immigrant sentiment.

After he signed up to work on the railway, Wong was most likely sent to Yale, BC, the furthest destination reachable by paddlewheeler up the Fraser River from New Westminster. The river was impossible to navigate north of Yale, where it narrows dramatically and becomes the wild and treacherous rapids of Hell's Gate, a site where many Chinese workers lost their lives. Wong rarely mentions the names of the towns and villages he travelled through and worked in, but there are sometimes clues in his writings. Andrew Onderdonk ran the Fraser Canyon railway construction project from Yale and built a large house in the town. Chinese crews lived in tents on the flats just downriver from Yale and were often sent upriver to work, walking as much as forty kilometres to other worksites. By 1885, much of the eastern part of the town became a thriving Chinatown which lasted well into the twentieth century, though no building of that original community remains standing today.

In his first diary entry after leaving Oregon, Wong writes in a tone of incredulity, "And they want this railway built across these high mountains, some two thousand miles!" If he was standing on the cliffs of the Fraser Canyon above Yale, looking upriver, he might well have been incredulous. The number of tunnels to be dug through solid granite, and the cliff faces to be blasted away, and the hundreds of thousands of tons of rock that would have to be moved must have been daunting to the strongest of men. Many might have thought to look elsewhere for work. Wong briefly shared that thought. In his next entry, he talks of a "city across the waters" where there is work loading ships and cutting lumber. Wong's granddaughter believes he was writing about Victoria. However, the thought that those jobs might have been easier than the work he was doing on the railway was quickly offset by the racism he feared he would have faced in Victoria. He had been told that the Chinese people there had been treated very badly, "some have said like dogs."

A letter written in 1885 to the Chinese merchants of Victoria and posted in the streets by the Anti-Chinese Association clearly demonstrated the extent of the racism festering in that city:

> Ship your coolies hence now, whilst you are given the chance. You are inimical to our institutions, laws and forms of government, defiant of our courts, subtle at evading taxation, evading our sanitary laws, and unwilling to assist in protecting our property from fire... The time has come for such an undesirable people to be banished from our land. Take our advice and leave whilst you have the chance of doing so peacefully, before an outraged people treat you as your conduct so deserves. If you oblige us to use force to rid ourselves of this scourge, the blame will rest on your own heads.

—The Anti-Chinese Association of Victoria, 1885[21]

Wong seems to believe that the racism in Victoria, like the racism he experienced in Oregon, was somehow more pernicious than what he would experience in the Fraser Canyon. This optimism is short-lived. Racial bias was everywhere in the province and very clearly embedded in the working conditions for Chinese workers employed by the CPR. They were paid one dollar per day, and with that dollar they had to buy their gear and their food, which for the most part consisted of rice and dried fish. White workers were paid up to $2.50 per day, and the railway provided their meals and supplies. The railway also provided help with medical care to white workers, while Chinese workers – who were being killed and injured in explosions and landslides, becoming sick with vitamin deficiencies, and freezing to death in the winter

---

21  David Chuenyan Lai, *Chinatowns: Towns within Cities in Canada* (Vancouver, BC: University of British Columbia Press, 1988). The word "coolie" was originally used to refer to physical labourers from Asia and South Asia. In this quote, and in the general language of the period, it was offensive and racist, as it is today. The inclusion of the word here is for the sake of historical accuracy, and no harm is intended.

months – were left to their own devices. An 1883 newspaper article in the *Yale Sentinel* reads:

> Here in British Columbia, along the line of the railway, the Chinese workmen are fast disappearing under the ground. No medical attention is furnished, nor apparently much interest felt for these poor creatures. We understand that Mr. Onderdunk [*sic*] declines interfering, while the Lee Chuck Co., that brought the Chinamen from their native land, refused…to become responsible for doctors and medicine.[22]

The reality of these circumstances soon begins to weigh heavily on Dukesang Wong. He has some difficulty understanding the Cantonese dialects of southern Guangdong, and worries that he's not an adequate spokesperson for his crew. While he questions his own ability to help his fellow Chinese workers, however, he doesn't call into question the role of the Chinese agents and contractors, several of whom handsomely profited from the misery of their countrymen. Thousands of the poverty-stricken men were indentured to these agents and never became free of their debts. Unable to pay their own passages from China, they borrowed money from the agents and remained indebted throughout their time in Gold Mountain. Many could, therefore, not save enough money to pay return fares and never returned to China. Though Wong doubts his abilities and finds his circumstances and those of his countrymen trying, he increasingly takes comfort in the company of his fellow workers and in the contact he makes with Indigenous people he meets on his journeys.

The significant gap between Wong's last 1882 diary entry, which begins "I despair," and the first entry of 1883, which begins "My soul cries out," becomes the norm between the end of 1882 and the summer of 1886. During these four years there are only six separate translated excerpts, and in them we meet a very different Dukesang Wong, a man now despairing and deeply affected by the conditions under which he and his fellow Chinese workers have to labour and live. Wong's granddaughter is unsure how many diary entries there were during those years, entries which, for any number of reasons, she chose not to translate. They certainly were the bleakest years of his writings. There is a darkness to his voice in many of these passages; it continues for three years.

"My soul cries out." Those first words of the fall of 1883 are a fitting introduction for what is to come. In the pages that follow he writes about

---

22   *Yale Sentinel* (1883), quoted in Berton, *The Last Spike*.

the source of this *cri du cœur*: the hardship and suffering of his people. His distress about the circumstances of his fellow workers confirms not just the details of that suffering, but the depth of his humanity and compassion for those whose misfortunes are greater than his own. The occasional allusions to the class of his upbringing, which appeared in earlier writings, seem to have been replaced by a deeper sense of community and a yearning for common good.

In several diary entries Wong writes about the illnesses ravaging the community, leaving many dead and others too ill to work. Some of this illness results directly from lack of fresh food. It wasn't possible to purchase medicines or fresh food on dollar-a-day wages, especially if workers' meagre pay was given directly to agents and contractors to pay off debts. While the meals provided by the railway company to white workers included meat and vegetables, Chinese workers had to provide for themselves, surviving on diets lacking in basic nutrition. Hundreds of Chinese workers died of scurvy, the result of a lack of vitamin C, and beriberi, a vitamin $B_1$ deficiency – even as those who sold them cheap polished rice and dried fish profited from the workers' inability to acquire or afford better and healthier food.

In a June 1883 telegram to Prime Minister John A. Macdonald, the Canadian High Commissioner to London, Sir Alexander Tilloch Galt, wrote, "Advise government allow no more Chinamen emigrate British Columbia as two thousand died past year from exposure accidents and other causes."[23] Although this number was exaggerated, the telegram makes it clear that the stories coming out of Canada had disturbed the British government. More disturbing is the sad fact that the high commissioner's recommendation for resolving the issue was not to correct the circumstances that resulted in the deaths, but to end Chinese immigration to Canada.

In this same section, between 1883 and 1886, Wong refers for the first time to turmoil in China. It is a subject to which he will later refer often. In an 1885 entry, he also writes for the first time about the new taxes being levied on the Chinese in Canada. He is, of course, referring to the now-infamous head tax enacted through the Chinese Immigration

---

23  An image of the original telegram can be found at the Critical Thinking Consortium (TC²) website, "Chinese Canadian Life on the Railway," tc2.ca/sourcedocs/uploads/history_docs/Chinese-Canadian%20History /Chinese-canadian-life-on-the-railway.pdf.

Act on July 20, 1885, over three months before the symbolic completion of the railway at Craigellachie, BC. While the act was in part a response to the pressure exerted by British Columbians and their politicians, the federal government in Ottawa was notably racist itself. In justifying the use of Chinese labour on the railway, for example, the prime minister said:

> At any moment when the Legislature of Canada chooses, it can shut down the gate and say, no more immigrants shall come here from China; and those in the country at the time will rapidly disappear and therefore there is no fear of permanent degradation by a mongrel race.[24]

It was clear in the months before the Last Spike was driven on November 7, 1885, in Craigellachie, that much of the work on the transcontinental railway was coming to an end. The Chinese had served their purpose, and it was time to stop this "unwanted" tide of immigrants. The head tax was intended as a disincentive, imposed only on Chinese immigrants entering the country. Initially it was set at $50, two months' wages for many workers. But by 1903 the tax had risen to $500, or about $12,500 in today's dollars. The American government had also been determined to slow migration from China, but approached the issue in a very different way. In 1882, following the completion of their railway, they passed the Chinese Exclusion Act, barring Chinese workers altogether. Canada followed Washington's lead several years later with the 1923 Chinese Immigration Act, excluding all Chinese immigrants but students and diplomats. The law remained in effect until 1947. Dukesang Wong questions Canada's imposition of the head tax with his usual logic, arguing that restrictions on Chinese workers made no sense in light of the amount of work still left to do. "There is much work to be done and not enough people to labour at it," he writes. "But the western people will not allow any to land here any longer, while they scold us for not working enough. How these acts wear my soul down to nothing."

Although there are few excerpts available to us from the difficult and tragic days of late 1883 to early 1886, what remains creates a vivid picture of the punishing work and crushing deprivation, racism, and death that Wong and his fellow Chinese workers experienced and witnessed. One curious diary entry in 1883 leaves us with a mystery.

---

24 Foundation to Commemorate the Chinese Railroad Workers in Canada (website), "The Ties That Bind," www.mhso.ca/tiesthatbind/HeadTax Exclusion.php.

While discussing the tensions between white and Chinese, especially concerning the Chinese being too ill to work, Wong asks, "How does anyone work when so ill? Many are killed when such words are spoken." Given the date of the entry, Wong may be referring to an incident that took place near Lytton, BC, on the night of May 10, when a gang of twenty white men entered railway camp number thirty-seven, set fire to a shack, and attacked the Chinese workers as they tried to escape the flames. One man, Ye Fook, was killed, and several others were beaten unconscious and badly injured. Refused treatment by a local white doctor, the injured men were carried to the Joss House, their place of worship in Lytton, where another worker died of his injuries a few days later.[25] It was believed that the attack was in retaliation for a confrontation between white and Chinese workers earlier that afternoon, when a foreman dismissed a sick worker without pay. It may explain the line "we are becoming more like dogs biting at one another." The situation left Dukesang Wong feeling helpless and useless.

Many months later, in the spring of 1885, a thaw made it possible to bury those who had died over the winter. Wong describes visiting the grave of his friend Wing Sun, who had died in "the hard, foodless days." It seems Wong walked to the grave to apologize that he hadn't been able to send the body 160 kilometres downriver to New Westminster and home to China to be buried with Wing Sun's ancestors. After a fellow worker criticizes him for bowing in the traditional Chinese way at the grave, Wong justifies the Confucian traditions of ancestor veneration. It is "imperative that we honour them," he writes.

Through all the sadness, violence, and tragedy, Wong manages to find wisdom, empathy, and poetry. In the middle of descriptions of men being killed for their complaints, and very sick men spending their days in opium dens, Wong is able to take pleasure in the arrival of spring and to look forward to visiting men who speak his dialect. His last thought of 1885, once again referring to the head tax and racism, contains one of the most striking observations in his diaries. "These mighty lands are great to gaze upon," he says, "but the laws made here are so small."

Chinese railway workers in Canada and the United States faced appalling, often inhumane circumstances. And it took more than a

---

25  Rev. Master Kōten, "A History of Healing in Lytton," Lions Gate Buddhist Priory (website), www.lionsgatebuddhistpriory.ca/ARCHIVE%20 articles/NL98A.pdf.

century for both countries to finally acknowledge their responsibility. Apologies were offered to citizens of Chinese heritage by both governments, the U.S. in 2006 and Canada in 2011, for institutional forms of racism such as Exclusion Acts and head taxes. Dukesang Wong's diary powerfully reveals the personal cost of this institutional persecution.

By 1886, Dukesang Wong was one of only a few Chinese workers still employed by the railway. Most Chinese men had been released earlier, and many found themselves in desperate circumstances. Wong briefly returns to New Westminster, where he is relieved to find fresh food. He observes, however, that it is probably "too late" for some of the men who "have been working their skin off, appearing more like skeletons." While the food recently arrived in New Westminster makes some of the men rejoice at their good fortune, Wong laments that others are beyond help.

A telegram sent in January 1885 to Sir Joseph-Adolphe Chapleau, the Secretary of State in Ottawa, from Clement Francis Cornwall, the Lieutenant-Governor of British Columbia, reads, "Respecting destitution among Chinese recently dismissed from Dominion railway works, request I may be informed by telegraph how far Dominion govt will be prepared to assist in extending immediate relief as considerable numbers of these wretched creatures are now reduced to actual starvation." [26] A report the following year by John Robson, the soon-to-be Premier of British Columbia, describes seeing homeless unemployed Chinese railway workers looking like skeletons and living in caves near Tilton Creek and other locations beside the Fraser and Thompson Rivers, eating dead and rotting fish that wash up along the shore.[27] Some of these caves can still be seen today.

Robson suggested moving the men to Victoria, albeit with the goal of expediting their deportation. But the government didn't act, and many more Chinese men, completely abandoned by the railway company and the government, died in Canada. Some of the men who could still be helped were rescued, fed, and tended to by Indigenous communities. Several married into these communities, including the Stó:lō Nation

---

26  Clement Francis Cornwall to Sir Joseph-Adolphe Chapleau, telegram, January 27, 1885, Library and Archives Canada, RG6-A-1, vol. 60, file 2235, items 10–11.

27  James Morton, *In the Sea of Sterile Mountains: The Chinese in British Columbia* (Vancouver, BC: J.J. Douglas, 1974), 107.

and the Nlaka'pamux Nation, and their descendants remain members of these nations today.

During his stay in New Westminster that summer, Wong makes note of the fact that he is sharing his living quarters "with three others who have come from a town that recently burned down." Although he doesn't name the town, he is certainly referring to Vancouver, sixteen kilometres west of him and only incorporated three months earlier. The CPR had acquired land in Vancouver, then called Granville, in order to run the railway to the west end of Burrard Inlet. On June 13, 1886, the brush on those lands was being cleared via burn-off in preparation for laying the track bed. A sudden wind arose, and the workers lost control of the fire. The town burned to the ground; all but a few buildings were destroyed. Most of the Chinese in Vancouver at that time fled to New Westminster, where a larger Chinese population had been established for several years. Once the townsite was rebuilt and renamed, and the transcontinental trains finally rumbled into the Vancouver terminus, the city's population exploded, soon dwarfing that of New Westminster.

During that same summer, Wong finally shares a cautious note of optimism. He suggests that circumstances for Chinese workers may be changing, though he adds that "the fortunes of our people need great care and guarding." He is acutely aware his people still live with the oppressive head tax and are treated by most whites in the province as undesirable citizens. However, that doesn't seem to prevent him from celebrating the recent arrival of tea. As the next undated entry appears to fall soon after the mention of the Great Vancouver Fire in mid-June, we can guess that the "feast day" Wong refers to is probably Dominion Day, July 1, 1886.[28] The workers had the holiday off, and Wong describes spending his time walking in the hills, devoting himself to his contemplations. His following sentence, like several others in the diaries, stands out: "I have pondered this fresh new land, yet it is a land already full of sadness." Fresh but sad, great but small – conclusions drawn from his thoughtful and careful observations of racism and injustice.

Wong then condemns what he believes is a growing and unseemly lust for gold that appears to have gripped so many of the people around him. The 1858 Fraser River Gold Rush had been the first to bring a

---

28 This national holiday was celebrated annually from 1879 to 1982, after which Parliament changed the name from Dominion Day to Canada Day.

significant number of Chinese to British Columbia, and smaller strikes in the years after continued to keep dreamers dreaming. In 1885, the year before Wong made this diary entry, gold was discovered in the Tulameen River at the mouth of Granite Creek by a local cowboy improbably named Johnny Chance. The Granite Creek Gold Rush began in the weeks that followed, and hundreds of gold-seekers, often unemployed former railway workers, both white and Chinese, flocked to the Tulameen Valley.

For Wong, the values that drive men to fight each other for gold are "peculiar." He quotes his teachers in arguing that only bad things will result from thoughtless greed. He claims to desire only enough for a home to which he can bring his betrothed, Lin. He implies that he wants nothing more than a productive and honourable life. He mentions Lin here for the first time since leaving China, a reminder that for Wong, the underlying goal of these years has been to prove himself worthy and establish a home for her.

As bad as things have been in Gold Mountain, Wong ends his entry from 1886 with a reminder that conditions in China may be worse. During the last twenty years of the nineteenth century, China suffered a losing war with France, defeat in a war with Japan, the imposition of European concessions in Shanghai, Guangzhou, Tianjin, and other cities, the defeat of the Boxer Rebellion by allied armies, endless local rebellions, droughts and starvation, and the constant harassment of towns and villages by bandits. Wong again refers to Lin, writing, "I am afraid for her life in the homeland since all of her family perished and she has little place to go." Although he gives no details regarding her family, we know that this was a dangerously violent and chaotic period in Chinese history, and men in the diaspora were well aware of the dangers to loved ones they left behind.

In a rare humorous anecdote from the summer of 1886, about a failed attempt by a young white thief to steal a carved piece of jade from Wong's friend, he relates a story that stands in stark contrast to the example of frontier justice he has earlier described. The friends offer the thief a dish of congee, and when he flees in terror, they are amused that white men always seem to be afraid of Chinese food. Wong's light tone and sense of humour is a dramatic shift from the misery and despair of the previous few years.

Wong's final entry of 1886 begins with a surprising announcement. He has decided to stay in New Westminster to make himself a home and establish a tailoring business there. This is the first we've heard anywhere in the translated diaries that Wong has any interest or skill in the work of tailoring. He seems to have made this decision in part because he observes a shortage of Chinese-style clothing available in New Westminster. He writes that no tailors in the town "cut the cloth in our manner," probably meaning that the tailors of European background don't, won't, or can't make the clothes the Chinese prefer to wear. In short, he recognizes an opportunity.

He goes on to write about making enough money to bring Lin to Gold Mountain, although no timeline is suggested. There is now affection in the way he speaks about her, and a note of admiration for the intelligence she shows in a letter despite her young age. Relying on the headstone dates at her gravesite in Vancouver, Lin would have been six years old in 1886. Accounting for errors in dating these entries, and even a possible error in the headstone date, potentially adding a few years to her age, it is still clear he is referring to a child, albeit one old enough to write a letter, a task she may have been required to fulfill by her guardians. In a reference to Lin's position as a second wife, he speaks of a previous relationship – "Ironic that I do not have a first, unless those brief moments with Su-Lin were first." Wong's granddaughter reports that he was known to have had a first marriage, or cohabitation, in China, and that the relationship produced a son. Neither this "wife" nor their son followed him to Canada, and no more is known about them. Wong says little about her and quickly dismisses the subject. While diaries can often contain personal and intimate details, Wong seems to consider these types of thoughts inappropriate, as evidenced by both his reaction here, and his earlier removal of diary pages related to the young student for whom he developed an attachment.

By the time he makes his first diary entry in 1887, Wong is again far from New Westminster and his notions of tailoring. He has been back working on the railway for seven months in a landscape he describes as hot, dry, and dusty, an environment he compares unfavourably to the cooler, more humid coast. Although he once again does not mention the names of nearby towns, we can conclude that he is most likely writing about the semi-arid landscape around Ashcroft and Savona in the BC Interior. Located 350 kilometres northeast of New Westminster, the area is often described as desert-like, and is home to tumbleweeds and cacti. We know from Canadian Pacific Railway records that the company continued to repair and upgrade track in this region for another three years after the supposed completion of the railway in 1885.

Though Wong admits he would prefer to leave the arid landscape, which seems to exacerbate his lung ailment, he hasn't yet saved enough for his future plans. His observation that no Chinese families need a tutor for their children leaves him musing again about his involvement in education. When he even wishes he knew English well enough to sit in on classes at the local school, he is in all likelihood referring to the first public elementary school in Ashcroft, which opened that same year and ironically was housed in a former CPR bunkhouse.[29] His reminiscences of the carefree days of his childhood and his life of privilege and education seem to coincide with, and even reinforce, his notion that it is time to change the path of his life.

His nostalgia does not last long, however, and he is probably back in New Westminster for the next entry in his diary, which he starts by acknowledging his good fortune that he was not part of a tragedy which saw the deaths of hundreds of men, according to his information. Again, he does not provide many particulars about this event, but the timing and the detail he does provide are enough to conclude that the disaster he speaks of is the Nanaimo mine explosion, which occurred on May 3, 1887. This tragedy still stands as the most deadly mine disaster in the history of British Columbia and the second-worst in Canadian history. The explosion caused the deaths of 150 men, including fifty-three unnamed Chinese workers. Incredibly, it wasn't until the following decade that a law was passed making it mandatory for businesses to keep records of the names of their Chinese workers. Wong's last thought in this entry is for the families of the men who died.

His comments in the final entry of the year take a more celebratory turn; he writes about a ship that has arrived filled with food and spices, tea, and rice enough to celebrate for a full year. Now that the tragedy at Nanaimo is a few months old, he appears more optimistic. Little does he know that shortly he will have much more reason to be positive about his life. The year 1888 will be one of his most significant.

---

29  Barbara Roden, "Golden Country: Past, Present, and Beyond: Chinatown," *Ashcroft-Cache Creek Journal*, August 23, 2016, www.ashcroftcachecreekjournal.com/our-town/golden-country -past-present-and-beyond-chinatown/.

# MY LIFE IS NOW GOOD

## Spring 1888

Today I met another man from my village. Although he is one of the common villagers, he was educated a little and is most interesting. He proposed that we join together to establish a business to make clothes for others. He was a tailor of known quality in our village. I can just barely remember some references to him in my earlier years at home. I suppose that I must establish a trade of my own if I am to earn my own respect and surely that of Lin – although I would also like to buy land and work on it farming vegetables and some livestock. But perhaps this is foolish, the result of too many dreams.

He proposes that I would not need to contribute much money for it, but rather, as I have little knowledge of the business compared to him, be under apprenticeship to him for two years and eventually become a partner when I have gained enough experience. He is much older than me and also wishes reassurance for his only son's survival – a very young son for a man his age.

*

I have agreed to Wong-Sun-Ling's proposition. Today I have invested twenty-three ounces of gold into this business of tailoring. Wong-Sun-Ling's shop is in the front part of his home very near the river, and the ships' supplies, he says, are extremely useful. The ceremony he contrived for the "blessings of the gods and driving out of devils" was strange and left my mind in awe, though I suppose he must adhere to his house's order.

*

## Late Autumn 1888

My life is now good. The tailoring work has been worthwhile and is of a good grade, for which we can hold our faces up. So many people desire garments that we do not have enough cloth to work with. Today I am departing for my homeland. My soul is excited and desires to reach our shores to bring Lin to me. It is well.

*

The journey has been hard on my poor body. It will be so weak when I visit the courts and will not make a good impression. How I wish those masters would not have to look upon me, this body of bones, but I have obtained an audience already and am unable to have any time to renew my poor weary self. Yet landing is good; feet on the land feels so stable after being wobbly so long.

## 1889

My land is beautiful to my eyes, and Lin has truly
blossomed to womanhood. She has been tenderly raised
and well taught the rules of Li and the orders of piety. In my
conversations with her guardians, they tell of her temper –
but what is to be expected from a child of a good house?
Today I have seen her beauty – extremely white compared to
my unworthy darkness now. How I wish the three months
were up and I could see her again, but this desire is truly
without patience. "Oh soul, when thou endures patiently." I
need to ensure I prevent this anxiety from becoming visible
to her guardians. I must be the honourable and controlled
man!

I also wandered through my village – though no longer
mine – and felt my regret at the passing of the memories of
my youth. My father's grave is sadly in need of care, as Lin
has not been allowed to travel there to tend to it. Tomorrow,
I will attend to it. But when I return to the Land of the
Golden Mountain, there will be no one left to see to its care.
If only my dear sisters could.

*

I am now an honoured man. I am now a real man also.
Lin is my wife – my wife. "I have bought bread and I have
been given red robes:[30] how happy I am to hold both in my
hands!" She protested the appropriate number of times, but
when I gazed upon her, her eyes were full of anticipation

---

30   See commentary for an explanation of these marriage traditions.

and not of fear. She would not take my hand, but from
one with careful propriety that is to be expected. I feel my
height to her smallness – her stature is small. It is good. My
patience is being tested, for my desire is present to me. If
only I had a home to take her to, rather than these poor
chambers!

## Spring 1892

Daily the business is becoming more prosperous, although
there are some that hesitate to enter this place, I am told,
because of the blue banner I must necessarily show in
respect to Sun-Ling's death. He was a very good man,
though somewhat lacking in education, but he knew a
great deal about this business. I have a heavy heart as, at
times, I do not fully know men's dress styles here, except my
own tastes. The white people have influenced some of our
ideas. My own dress is only of the old order, not of this new
adaptation.

*

Today I gained an evening position teaching some of the
children in the community. Once again, my mind is active
in knowledge. Lin-Ying[31] is devoted to the care of several
children whose mothers have to labour. My heart is glad
that she enjoys this land, for her regret in not producing
sons has lately silenced her usual talk. But it is natural and

---

31  Lin and Lin-Ying are the same person. It was common to give a person
a "courtesy" name, also called a "style" name, as they get older. This
name was added with a hyphen to the person's given name.

may be for the best now, for I could not have more mouths to feed as yet. Perhaps in another year I will be truly joyful.

## Late Autumn 1892

Now I have a great heavy heart. I cannot sit still very long to write, but must do so. Lin has been very ill with a skin disease and fever. She has had a miscarriage during her illness, and I am not able to console her. Struggling for life has been hard for one so young and pampered, even though she has been quite worthy in her attempts to adjust and be a true wife. She will not permit me to aid in her despair. Her nearest guardian has advised me to allow her to rally herself for a period, but it is with great heaviness in my soul that I now watch her. I would like to comfort her, but she blames her circumstances and her fate. How I long for those ordered days at home when my dear mother would have been able to console her in a woman's way! My business does well; if only my family were to be so equalled!

*

So much disease spreading. My meagre knowledge cannot help, yet they turn to me for aid. Herbal tea will cool the body but not perform miracles for the diseased skin!

## Summer 1894

Today I have great joy and also great sorrow. We are to be parents soon, I am told. I am now contented. My joy, however, must be suppressed, as this afternoon I heard of unrest in the homeland, in the villages around the court. This news is troubling, as there is serious talk of ridding our homeland of the foreigners. In many cases, it would be good, but foreigners also bring new and stimulating knowledge, and such an expulsion would not be appropriate. All knowledge needs new light in order to see even greater truth in that knowledge. This saddens my soul ...

## Early Spring 1895

"One joy dispels a hundred cares," and my cares are surely dispelled. The name of Wong will continue. I am impatient that the month is so long, for I wish to present my child. How my virtuous masters would look down as they heard of my impatience, but my joy is great. How I wish to tell all those who pass, but I must control myself ...

*

Much honour has been given to me this year, and I am humbled to receive such bounty. The boy[32] is growing into manhood and is doing well in the trade. He will also become literate and tell his own children about the wisdom of the Sage, which I have tried to impart to him. My child is strong and healthy. The order is oh, so good. Further honour has been bestowed upon me as headmaster of the community, and this next month I will start to teach several

---

32  The son of Wong's business partner. See commentary for further explanation.

children. They have allotted several rooms to my devices for a school. My knowledge is being made useful for our people.

## Autumn 1895

My precious wife, how the times are acting well for us both! How can anybody expect me to remain aloof and controlled from our son and from you when both of you are so joyous to my eyes? Yet you become angry with me in such degrading tones when I desire to demonstrate my affection for you. Mother of my son, I realize that it is not within the bounds of propriety that I walk evenly with you and show my care, but you carry a double load now. It is impossible for me not to show my feelings. Let them laugh! It is not in my soul to be concerned over others' laughter. I cannot follow their traditions of degrading or ignoring their women in the sight of others.

*

The order cries out for justice and re-ordering in these days of little work. So many of our people are coming to this land, coming with dreams to build their own home here, away from the turmoil in the homeland. So many, with so little, but so great in need. Many come from the southern regions of China, Kwangtung[33] province, and they search for ingredients to make their own dishes, not thinking that this land cannot grow the vegetables they can in their home villages. Accepting the changing land here is very hard for

---

33  Now known as Guangdong.

them, as indeed it is also for my meagre mind. I wonder at their wailing, however, because they denounce their trials so loudly, and are so rude to some who have come here earlier. Yet I, too, have come earlier, but they give great deference to me. It is not proper either way.

## Late Spring 1896

In my thoughts, I have offended the great ancestors' teachings and desires. I am joyful for my second son's full month celebration, yet I want a precious daughter, a girl I can enjoy. Sons are in the good order, but to them I must appear a ruler of the house and cannot participate in their intimate lives. People have already said that I indulge my sons too much and will spoil them for any worthwhile deeds and work. The ancestors have taught that indulgence to children must be from people other than their father, or they will not have respect for me. Yet I wonder how one can respect without any soul attached to the acts of respect. I believe that my way, showing them all that I care, will also gain respect. How I wish for a guide in my new life here; I am sad that I cannot have the wisdom of the masters here in this changed life.

## Late Summer 1896

We have recently been honoured in our home by the presence of Chang Ly Heong, the great leader of the area of Kwangsi.[34] He tells of the turmoil in our homeland and would wish us all to return to help correct the ways of the warlords. He spoke of the increased fervour against the white missionaries in the homeland and his own passionate desires to be rid of the westerners.

He is an honourable man, but I fear that he is not taught by the ways of the Sage. Confucius has said that we all, people together, should learn the best ways from each other. Wisdom, it is written, transcends different villages, different lands both north and south, east and west. The truth is knowledge, and knowledge is good in the order of living. Learn the good others have to bring to you, and reject the unworthy. All the things we have learned from visitors, yet Chang would have us be rid of other people from outside our land.

I cannot return to any home village. Lin is too busy with the care of the boys, and there would not be time for her to make clothing to fill the promised orders. Also, where would I go for shelter? And I cannot believe that there is real truth in the gossip brought here by the newly arrived people. They are not learned persons, though I wish that learned people would come. I must think deeply before acting ...

1897

It is a strange twist of the order of life that the people of our homeland press for the exclusion of westerners, calling them barbaric and white devils, accusing them of taking land and

---

34   Now Guangxi.

life from China's wealth, and berating them for bringing
opium to our people – while in this Land of the Golden
Mountains, the westerners make rules to control our movements and prevent further ships from China and Japan
landing here, call us savages and non-Christians, accuse us
of taking from them positions of work which they refuse
to do, say we take their money and return it to China, and
burn down the opium houses, into which they also come.
It is indeed a strange land and a very strange time to live.

The adversity here remains and grows. Our people are
not wise enough to allow time for contemplation and care
for their children. The young must work and for little food
and money. To see such young ones cry out with their eyes
at the sadness they must surely feel is not to be borne. My
boys also want to earn money as their companions do, but
they are so young. What of childhood enjoyment? I cannot.

## 1899

My children are Chinese people! Seong Yee would have
them become English, enter the citizenship of the English.
As an example, Yee says. My thoughts are in turmoil. Some
say we should all become English. The western ways are all
so easily adopted, yet I would not adopt them all. I wish for
my children one day to return to China and establish themselves, to hold good names in our homeland. We must not
be buried on foreign land!

*

No arguments in any case can persuade those mindless people. They say we must ask to be citizens in this land again and again. They even want to buy papers to do so. Such impropriety shames me, and our ancestors will surely not be told such thoughts!

1900

Japanese people are treated with great deference by the westerners. Their ways are so much like ours, yet there is no such thought for us to share fresh food and cloth, to have stone buildings in which to teach the children.

*

The Indians have great ways to obtain food – meat from the wild animals. Sing has brought some deer meat from one such Indian family, tasting wild, but meat still. I have in return a chicken, saved for our summer feast, but it is necessary. I hope they will understand our meaning. Fowls are so close to the heavens. I wish we could also have sent oranges, so colourful and cheerful, in return.

# THE ORDER IS OH, SO GOOD

Dukesang Wong's earlier notion about becoming a tailor must have seemed increasingly attractive to him after yet another year of hard labour on the railway. In the spring of 1888, he meets a man who proposes that very idea. It is tempting to imagine a conversation between him and the man, Wong-Sun-Ling, whom he had just met, a conversation in which Wong might have mentioned his unfulfilled desire to become a tailor. Interesting, the man might have said, I'm a tailor and I'm looking for a partner. Wong did not jump at the opportunity immediately. He appears to have waited a day or two, allowing himself time to consider another possible option. He writes of a second, previously unexpressed, interest; his desire be a farmer, to raise livestock and grow vegetables.

During his ten months doing railway work in and around Ashcroft and on the plateau lands along the Thompson River, Wong would have come into regular contact with Chinese market gardeners who were well known for their farming skills, especially for their innovations with irrigation and crop rotation. After being abandoned by the CPR in 1885, many men turned to the land for their survival, falling back on what they knew best from their previous lives in China. Curiously, market farming in British Columbia had been left largely to the Chinese because, like laundering and cooking, it was considered women's work. For years, both before and after railway construction, Chinese market gardeners in several parts of the province played a significant role in food production. The success of these farmers was noted by Sir Matthew Baillie Begbie, Chief Justice of the Supreme Court of British Columbia, in his testimony before the Royal Commission on Chinese Immigration in 1885. In that testimony he remarked, "I do not see how people would get on here at all without Chinamen [*sic*] ... They are the model market gardeners of the province, and produce the greater part of the vegetables grown here."[35]

Having very probably spent time among these farmers while grading railway beds and repairing tracks, Wong might have come to see their lives as idyllic. He would perhaps have admired their independence and envied the satisfaction that came from working the earth and growing food. However, he also acknowledges that his farming fantasy may be unrealistic, and within days of their initial conversation, he accepts the tailor's offer. He agrees to invest twenty-three ounces of gold in the business and to apprentice himself to Wong-Sun-Ling for two years, after which he will become a partner.

The shop was set up in the front part of Wong-Sun-Ling's house in New Westminster, probably on Front Street, overlooking the river and the wharfs. It was there, along the waterfront street, that the city's first Chinatown had grown into the largest on the provincial mainland. "The Swamp," a boggy piece of land further along the river that was prone to flooding, became a second Chinatown. Both neighbourhoods were destroyed in the Great Fire of 1898 and only partially rebuilt. By the 1940s, all traces of these two Chinatowns had disappeared and to this day there is little indication in the city that early Chinese settlers were ever a significant part of its population.

After more than ten years of diary keeping in China, struggling with the loss of his parents and his family's reputation, wandering the country seeking tutoring positions, and almost ten years in the Land of the Golden Mountains, struggling with hunger, sickness, and racism while working himself into exhaustion, Dukesang Wong's fortunes now appear to have turned. It will take time for him to trust this turn. Nevertheless, he finds the tailoring enterprise "worthwhile," and, finds he can be proud of the products of his labour. Then, as he has done before in the middle of a diary entry, he makes a surprising announcement, writing, "Today I am departing for my homeland."

---

35    Government of Canada's Royal Commission on Chinese Immigration, with Sir Joseph-Adolphe Chapleau and John Hamilton Gray, *Report of the Royal Commission on Chinese Immigration: Report and Evidence*, Sessional Paper no. 54a (Ottawa, ON: Government of Canada's Royal Commission on Chinese Immigration, 1885), 75, www.canadiana.ca /view/oocihm.14563/3?r=0&s=1.

In the fall of 1888, Wong leaves New Westminster and travels to China. While the primary reason for the journey is to meet with Lin's guardians and arrange her move to Canada, he also writes that his weakness and physical condition are an embarrassment and impediment to the audience he will have with some "masters" of the courts. He doesn't elaborate or mention this audience again, but it would be reasonable to guess that he used part of his time there to sue for a return of the family's good name.

Confusions about dates and Lin's age appear again in this section of the diary. While it reads as though he married her in China, his granddaughter is quite sure that Lin left the country and lived for a while on Vancouver Island with her guardians before marrying Wong and moving to New Westminster. Adjusting timelines slightly, it is likely that she was between eight and ten when Wong arrived in China. After seeing her only briefly, he is required to wait three months before seeing her again. During that period, he visits his childhood village and his father's grave. Though he is not yet forty, there is something world-weary in his brief description of this time – or perhaps it is simple nostalgia and regret for a world now lost to him. According to family history, it was during this visit to the homeland that Wong arranged the emigration of Lin and her guardians from China to Canada to await the marriage.

According to Wanda Joy, the wedding took place two or three years later in Victoria, BC. Wong describes a few of the memorable moments in the traditional ceremony. His mention of having bought bread is probably a reference to the traditional bridal pastries provided by the groom, the most popular one of which was the "wife cake." The red robes he carried were the traditional Chinese wedding robes. His pride at becoming a married man is evident, as is his yearning for the wedding night. This brief entry, possibly made sometime in 1891–1892, is once again short on detail. Lin was probably thirteen or fourteen when she married Wong, while he would have been close to fifty, and their marriage came about through an arrangement made years before, when she was a toddler. But in most circles of Imperial Chinese society, neither the difference in age nor the age of the bride would have been all that unusual.

The early 1890s marks a period of domesticity in Wong's life, the subject of many subsequent diary entries. He also writes about the growing prosperity of his tailoring business, although he worries that unlike his late business partner he does not understand the newest fashions and has difficulty adapting to the influences of western clothing. Wong often wore a traditional changshan, a robe-like long shirt, with a Mandarin-collared jacket, until after the turn of the century. During this time he may also have worn the queue, a long strand of braided hair required by law in Manchu China.

In the summer of 1894, Wong announces that he and Lin will have a child. He is also concerned with news from China. He writes that there is talk of ridding the country of foreigners, but he believes that knowledge flourishes with openness to other cultures and new ideas. Much of the trouble and unrest Wong refers to in 1894 was the response to yet another colonial war, this time with Japan. After losing earlier wars with Britain and France, China was now faced with the Sino-Japanese War, a war they would also lose.

Nine months later, Wong is anxious to tell the world about the birth of his first child with Lin and to present him to the community, but he must abide by the Chinese tradition of "sitting the month," a period of thirty days of adjustment during which neither child nor mother leaves the confines of the home. It was a two-thousand-year-old tradition to which both Wong and Lin would have been committed. Only after a month is the child officially a person and the celebration of the birth takes place. Throughout the rest of the diary, this son will be called Second Son. Wong's first son was from a mysterious earlier relationship, and neither mother nor son ever left China.

By the spring of 1895, Wong has more reason to feel blessed. He is now the headmaster of the community Chinese school. He also writes about the son of his late business partner, whom he calls "the boy"; he had taken on parental responsibility for the young man and is pleased with his maturity and literacy. In addition, he is happy about his own infant son's good health. Wong can now write, "The order is oh, so good."

It was frowned upon to show affection for wife and family in many cultures in the nineteenth century, including traditional Chinese culture, but Wong finds it difficult to behave in traditional ways when he is with them. He argues that ignoring women in public is degrading to them and that walking together is especially important now, given that Lin carries a "double load" – no doubt a reference to her second pregnancy. While Wong remains largely true to his Confucian convictions, the world is changing, and he must adapt. He observes that many newcomers to his community struggle with change and are unable to adapt.

A few months later he admits to feeling another period of internal conflict, this time about his sons. He believes his affection for them is constrained by a traditional authoritarian role, denying him a place in what he refers to as their "intimate lives." He wrestles with the idea that showing children affection can result in lack of respect for their father, and ultimately concludes that paternal attention, love, and even indulgence can in fact help foster respect. He finds himself wishing he had access to the wisdom of the masters to help him navigate this "changed life." Change will prove to be a central preoccupation for the remainder of Wong's diaries.

Wong's summer 1896 diary entry begins with the announcement that Chang Ly Heong has been visiting British Columbia. This name is a varia- tion of Li Hongzhang. Li had been one of China's most powerful political and military figures prior to the country's loss in the Sino-Japanese War. As advisor to the Dowager Empress Cixi, he had presided over much of China's diplomatic relationships with the rest of the world. After China's loss to Japan, Li was demoted to a provincial governorship, but within a few months Cixi had chosen him to represent the Imperial Court at the coronation of Tsar Nicholas II in Moscow. He then continued on from Russia representing China's interests in Europe and North America, arriving in British Columbia in the summer of 1896. If he visited any Chinese communities outside Vancouver, New Westminster would surely have been among them. The more likely scenario, though, would put Wong among the six thousand Chinese who travelled from communities across the Pacific Northwest to greet Li in Vancouver. By 1896, the city was booming and had grown to be the largest in the province. The visit was reported in newspapers around the world.

China's many political upheavals had begun to preoccupy its worldwide diaspora. Li Hongzhang's 1896 visit certainly inspired much philosophical and political reflection in Dukesang Wong. His few entries over the next couple of years are often focused on complex questions of Chinese sovereignty, nationalism, and the erosion of traditional Confu- cian values in a rapidly modernizing country. While Wong admires Li, he clearly has serious doubts about the Chinese diplomat's opposition to foreign influence in China. He argues that Confucianism teaches that wisdom transcends nations and that rejection of foreign influence will result in a homeland as intolerant and "barbaric" as North America.

Although much of his writing during this time reflects what he calls his good fortune, it is worth noting that even in 1897 he is still writing about racism and listing racist behaviour directed at the Chinese in North America by "westerners." He seems to have concluded that ignorance is one of the foremost consequences of the intolerance and racial hatred he has witnessed in the New World. He fears the same result for the homeland. It is odd, though, that he seems almost naive about the devastating impact colonialism has had on China, although he is willing to acknowledge the terrible consequences of the introduction of opium. And he finds it ironic that the racism and rejection he has experienced every day from whites in North America is now directed at "white devils" in China.

Two short diary entries from 1899 express Wong's concern about a growing opinion in his community in favour of the adoption of western ways and for fraudulent efforts to gain citizenship in Canada and the United States, often by means of buying false papers. These documents created what came to be called "paper sons" and "paper daughters." Immigrants bought and carried these forged papers, which identified them as relatives of legal immigrants in Canada or the United States. Any other access was either blocked by acts of exclusion or made increasingly difficult by head taxes. The Canadian government was months away from raising its hated head tax from $50 to $100, and four years later raised it to $500.

Wong struggles with the argument put forward by some in his community that citizenship in Gold Mountain is a goal worth seeking by any means. For Wong, even the legal process meant going begging, a humiliation not worth the benefit. He also expresses his dismay that the Japanese in Gold Mountain were treated better than the Chinese – as only the Chinese were subject to head taxes and to legislated exclusion. Of course, had he lived until World War II, Wong would have seen Japanese families rounded up and sent to internment camps in both Canada and the United States. In his last entry for the year 1900, and for the second time in the diaries, he writes about "the Indians," admiring their skills and generosity. That generosity must have contrasted starkly with the treatment Indigenous and Chinese peoples received from most of the white population of both Gold Mountain countries.

# THE FINAL JOURNEY HOMEWARD

1901

It is challenging to my soul to hear of the rebellion at home.
So much useless honour being thrown away is surely disturbing for every knowledgeable person, and it is against
our long civilization and all our great teachings. They say
the city is being burned and that many are dead – killed
before their lives existed. Barbarism has finally returned.
The white people have brought us some good in their
books and have appeared friendly. Often I have said that
knowledge is universally good and its challenges must add
in some way to the good order of truth. It is such rebellions
that have caused our great sages to write of order, peace,
stillness, tranquility – but no, common people have proved
themselves again to shun all and to listen to their unsavoury
gods of destruction and disruption.

This not only offends my soul but also my mind, for the
children. They will lack the knowledge of the westerners in
our homeland, however many there are. The white people
in our land mingle with us and share their books with us
while here they separate us as if we were dishonourable. It is
curious that some of the barbaric whites are so unclean, yet
they believe us unclean and treat us not as men. But I have

99

ceased to desire to return to my village, for I am now of this house, but I am also greatly saddened, for now I can only hope to be buried in a nameless land.

## 1903

Our community leaders have united to form the Benevolent Association, something I have often hoped for the people of our land in this country. They do me great honour in their esteemed judgment by calling upon me to be a leader – in fact, to be the president. It is a great honour to have this position, for I know of several who would be better than this meagre person. How much the boys now can hold their father in honour, even though their grandfather was dishonoured.

*

Today I have been chosen to lead all of the Wong name. It is truly a great and burdensome honour. My children will indeed bear a good and venerable name to prosperity. I hope my grandchildren will not think of me in dishonour and will someday return to their home.

*

Rumour has it that Sun Yat-sen is coming to this land – may he live to do so.

## Early Winter 1905

Sing is ten years old, Third Son is nine years old, Fourth Son is four years old, but no baby girl. The mother of my sons also now wishes for a daughter, as I have caught her murmuring to Third Son about not being female. People would surely laugh at us both for our ways.

*

They have brought Heong Sing[36] from the inland area to harbour him against the westerners, who are crazy with unreasonable hate. Heong is not well, mostly sick in body, as he received many beatings for his mild protests. A gang of white robbers beat him nearly dead, and he will surely not live much longer. I write this as my soul cries out for wise decisions. Heong is not of my family, but he is one of our people – yet he would lead those poor beggars to work with great illusions. He cannot convince these newly arrived that the inlanders treat our people less well than here in this town. The sewer cleaners are better treated. Heong Sing is not a bright man to act in this manner, although I can only have pity for him in this condition. Lin nurses him, giving him condolence at having no son to carry his name, she says.

## Autumn 1907

We are in good fortune, as the summer has brought much food. The vegetables have had a large yield – no wonder, for Lin cares for them so studiously. The cycle is good to this family, as even the boys are well and strong, stuffing themselves full of chicken and fish. My own eyes are clean, unlike so many of my age, and I am joyful in these days. My only

---

36   No information about this person has been found.

desire is that my father and mother would be here with us to lead the boys and teach them their wisdom. My own experience would be greatly enhanced if the boys had the wisdom of their grandparents to guide their ways. I do, nevertheless, delight in being able to forego the traditional control of myself and watch the boys play and grow. They are now being taught so much that is new that I cannot explain the reasons and give answers to their questions.

## Spring 1908

Fifth Son, the fat one, is now with us and delighted the greatly honoured Sun Yat-sen today. Such an honourable person, but such great humbleness as to give us shame for the pride we take in our little achievements. He is also sad and weary for his homeland. The driving soul is with him still, in his eyes, yet I can sense a weariness. He has been working continuously for such a long time – he even writes by the light of candles, straining his eyes, now nearly without sight. The promised government elected by all the people has yet to be realized. All the talk has gone, like mist before the sun, into nothing. Reform has been mouthed, but some would reform with guns in their hands. Wan Siguay, Sun has said, has built a powerful but corrupt army, plundering lands and stealing from even those who have nothing. The Dowager Empress has no power to sift through her fingers, and men will not follow her madness.

We here have gathered our meagre fortunes together and celebrated the honoured Sun's visit, but can give little to help his ideas become reality in a corrupted and disputed homeland.

## Winter 1908

Word has come of the death of the Dowager Empress. Her unfortunate son, so young, now sits on an unguided throne. There is much discussion about a constitutional Imperial court – a curious idea, because the Emperor can have learned advisors, and the learned can govern together, but put an emperor and a government of learned men to rule together – this is extremely curious!

## Early Spring 1911

The new arrivals held a meeting today to obtain an opinion from all of us, to convey our feelings and thoughts to Sun. There is talk of ending the Imperial court, and I cannot speak, for the turmoil in my mind wonders about the differing age, this new age, so much. Sun is a scholar, yet he has written that we must do more than advise the new young Emperor Puyi or challenge his advisors: the people must completely reform the governmental system that has been established for so long in an orderly manner. I can only think that many will suffer and perish, and that the order of life has become so strange in the homeland.

## Autumn 1911

My heart is light, for the mother of my sons will soon have another baby. How we have wished for a daughter! But we must keep our thoughts to ourselves, as even Lin will not talk of her pregnancy.

*

Today I learned that the great Sun Yat-sen has written of
a new governing order for our homeland. How I desire to
have conversation with the scholars about all their reflec-
tions on these new orders!

## Autumn 1912

A great day of feasting for our household, and several days
of even greater feasting in these weeks of harvest – Sixth Son
has become a person, reaching his full month feast on this
day, and our homeland is a country now governed by elected
leaders under the honourable Sun, a worthy head man.

The news says that western companies have been
removed from control over their railways and lands, and
taxes on them have ceased to exist, yet all this has been
done with much slaughter and turmoil. I have not joined in
the celebrations with full, open heart. Our ancestors have
taught reason, for through discussion with men of ability to
reason, much can be gained and little need be violently lost.

I also think now of my father's disgraced name and
that there is no hope, even through my sons, to restore our
family name to its once honoured state. In such revolt, how
can the order of life hold any meaning to the young, who so
mindlessly overturn it? Sun Yat-sen promised that he would
send word to us of our home villages, but it has been many
months and many ships have landed without his writing.

Perhaps I am becoming too old now to understand
the new ideas. I hope my sons will be able to carry on my
thoughts.

## 1914

Second Son was all in a fervour today, as we have word of
great wars in the homeland as well as in the western lands.
He wants to return to our home village, yet I fear his youthful
ideals, which could lead to misguided and unpondered deeds.
Have we not already been told of the treatment of soldiers
under a general arising from the peasantry in the south? Have
we not been already told that the soldiers are not controlled,
pious men, but that they harm the people and steal from
them? It has been said. I cannot convince Sing that his
knowledge is not sufficient to do anything with significance.
His ideas rage in his head and even carry to Third Son.

*

Sadness fills so much of me, yet joy is also in my soul in
these warm days. Second Son has left with the missionary
ship to journey to the homeland. His going leaves us with
such heavy hearts, for I already feel that I shall not hear his
laughter again. I have allowed his journey, as a man must
cease to linger in his home when searching for knowledge,
though I greatly fear his search will lead him to much
physical pain. Third Son departs soon to enter university
in the eastern part of these lands. His abilities in learning
are high, and I am humbled by the honour which he has
achieved in attending university. There is a zeal in his desire
to help the ill and ailing, and it is unworthy of me to wish to
hold him here for fear the westerner's government will send
him to fight in France like so many others. It is said that the
old ways cannot always last, and that people must change

and be continuously renewed. I have even taught this – yet I fear that I cannot change enough for this new world.

## Spring 1916

Many of our people have chosen to fight in the European war in order to learn the newest methods of warfare. They say the techniques developed in the western world are better than those we have learned, and knowledgeable fighters are greatly needed in the homeland.

How it saddens my heart that our homeland has changed so much and that turmoil has separated our people, and they become easily overtaken by other, different people!

## Late Summer 1916

Another son – but he is the seventh and a good omen for our meagre lives. Second Son will journey back to this land: truly we will have a good autumn this year.

## Autumn 1918

It is still the feast of the full moon. I am doubly blessed, for in my desires, I have both prayed to the Christian god and allowed incense to be burned in our garden. My fate now has provided a daughter, a precious eighth child, a great joy for all this house! Her brothers will know this goodness and take care of her, loving her. She has come in my old age, a joyous sign, and she will be able to bring me pride, I know! It is good. Her brothers are men now, so she will be assured a good life. She will look after Lin when I leave these lands for the final journey homeward.

# THE OLD WAYS CANNOT LAST

In his first diary entry of 1901, Wong turns his thoughts back to China. By the latter years of the nineteenth century, the country had suffered the humiliation of giving up both power and territory to several foreign governments, losing wars to better-equipped, modernized English and French armies. And despite the efforts of the Self-Strengthening Movement begun by Li Hongzhang and others, the Chinese armies were no match for the superior forces of Japan in the Sino-Japanese War. Foreign concessions had been given up in major cities including Guangzhou, Shanghai, Beijing, and Tianjin.

Along with the political and military presence of foreign nations came the spread of Christianity, and with that combination came resistance. By the end of the 1890s, a significant number of rebels had joined forces to rid their country of foreigners and the religions they brought with them. Many of the fighters were peasants who had suffered through famine and natural disasters and had little to lose. The rebel numbers grew significantly and began attacking and killing foreigners, including missionaries. They became known to Europeans as the Boxers, named for their martial arts exercises.

The Boxer Rebellion took place mainly between 1900 and 1901. The rebels entered Beijing, surrounded the foreign territorial concessions, and kept the delegations isolated and virtually imprisoned for several weeks. It was then that the Dowager Empress gave her blessing to the rebellion, declaring war on all foreign powers in the country. In response an international force made up of armies from eight nations marched its way to Beijing, captured the city, and demanded yet more concessions from the weary country. The failure of the rebellion was another step in the fall of the Qing Dynasty, gone by 1911, and the rise of the new China.

During the two bloody years of the rebellion, many thousands died. The news spread quickly in overseas Chinese communities. Dukesang Wong was deeply disturbed by what he heard about the events in China. He opposed the rebellion, calling it barbaric. He returns to his argument that the foreigners had brought much good to China, and that it was in opposition to just such rebellions that the sages had written about peace and tranquility. Informed as it was by the privilege of his youth, it is difficult not to see his position as somewhat blinkered to the poverty and despair that drives such revolutions. Rather, he is alarmed by the prospect of the impending absence of what he believes to be a benevolent European influence in China, especially because he has come to believe there was precious little to be learned from the cultural influences of Gold Mountain. In his view, rather than share their knowledge with the Chinese as equals, which he seems to believe was the case in China, North American white culture held the Chinese in contempt and excluded them. It is worth noting that at the time of this diary entry, Dukesang Wong has been in North America for twenty years.

Dukesang Wong's granddaughter chose to include only three short entries from 1903. The first entry announces what may have been the unofficial establishment of a Benevolent Society in Wong's community of New Westminster. Wong writes that community leaders and China-town merchants gathered to form the Chinese Benevolent Association, though records indicate that it did not officially join the continent-wide Chinese Consolidated Benevolent Association (CCBA) until 1915. The dates, however, coincide exactly with similar actions taken by the Seattle Chinese community just two hundred kilometres to the south.

Wong takes pride, moderated by his usual modesty, in being elected local president of this early version of the later CCBA and, during the same year, in being chosen to lead a local branch of the Wong Association. Wong Association branches still exist in several North American cities,[37] as do many other Chinese name associations across the continent. These associations still do much of the same work as the CCBA, though with a particular focus on the kinship established by having the same family name.

In a single sentence in the final passage of 1903, Wong announces that the revolutionary leader Sun Yat-sen is rumoured to be coming to British Columbia. No doubt aware of ever-present threats to Sun's life, he adds, "may he live to do so." During his sixteen years of revolutionary activity from 1895 to 1911, Sun was in exile, visiting North America on several occasions, sometimes in secret. In this 1903 entry, Dukesang

---

37  Wong Association branches still exist in Vancouver, Montréal, Toronto, Edmonton, and Calgary, and in most major U.S. cities.

Wong is probably referring to Sun's expected 1904 trip to the U.S. There is no record of a visit to Canada during that time.

The maltreatment of Chinese in communities throughout the western regions of both Canada and the U.S is well known and well documented. Beatings and property destruction were common in both countries, including lynchings and massacres in the U.S. Though Wong argues that the Chinese were treated better in "this town," meaning New Westminster, the 1907 Vancouver race riots occurred a few kilometres away just over a year later. More than a thousand white citizens attacked both Chinatown and Japantown, beating residents, smashing windows, and starting fires. In a late 1905 entry, Wong writes of taking in a family friend named Heong Sing after he was badly beaten for organizing protests demanding civil rights for the Chinese community in British Columbia. Where these protests and beatings took place isn't mentioned, but Wong writes that the treatment of the Chinese is much worse further inland where "the westerners ... are crazy with unreasonable hate."

Wong doesn't share many more details about the man, other than to express sympathy for him. Heong may have been sought after by authorities and seemed to have nowhere else to go. He was probably one of the thousands of men who made up the "bachelor society" of Chinese workers. The ratio of Chinese men to women at this time in Canada was twenty-eight to one.[38] Because of poverty in China and head taxes in Canada, which by this time had risen to $500 per person, the majority of Chinese men were unable to bring wives and families to Canada. Many stayed in the country to earn money to send home; some never saw their families again. Wong was certainly aware of the good fortune with which he was blessed. He is grateful for his family, for their good health, for his own good health, and for the success of his business. He is not shy about acknowledging this good fortune in the pages of his diary.

Spring 1908 brings one of the most intriguing entries in Dukesang Wong's fifty years of diary keeping, the announcement that a fifth son, a child he calls "the fat one," is the newest member of the family, and that the baby "delighted the greatly honoured Sun Yat-sen today." Conventional wisdom would have us believe that Sun Yat-sen was not in

---

38  Jeremy Luedi, "The Long Shadow of Canada's Chinese Head Tax," True North Far East (website), truenorthfareast.com/news/chinese -head-tax-canada-legacy.

Canada in 1908, and certainly not in New Westminster. However, Wong devotes most of the remainder of the entry to an intimate and sympathetic picture of Dr. Sun. What makes the entry especially intriguing is the familiarity with which he describes the man. First the reference to the baby, then the description of Sun working late into the night by candlelight. He observes that Sun is sad and weary but still has a fire in his soul and in his failing eyes. The detailed picture Wong paints suggests that a gathering may have been held in the Wong house, and that Sun was an overnight guest. Wong's leadership of the Benevolent Society would have made him an obvious host for such a distinguished visitor.

Most histories of the time suggest that Sun made only three visits to Canada, the first in 1897, followed by two more in 1910 and 1911, though there is no public record of a visit to the city of New Westminster during any of those three years. There is also no public record of a visit in 1908. It is, of course, possible that a mistake was made with dates, either in the original diary or in the translations, but another possible explanation for Wong's 1908 entry is that Dr. Sun did, indeed, visit the city that year. We know that he was in the United States in 1907–1908. We also know that he often travelled in secret, under an assumed name with a false passport, both for his own safety and for the safety of those he visited.

Sun was certainly known to have reached out to sympathetic Chinese communities within reach of Vancouver. In 1910 he spent almost a week in Ashcroft, British Columbia, a town with a significant Chinese population, though smaller than the numbers in New Westminster. Dr. Sun raised thousands of dollars in the cities and towns of British Columbia for the revolutionary cause of overthrowing the Qing Dynasty, and there is little reason to think that he would not have spent time with the supportive community in New Westminster. Wong is disappointed, however, that they were unable to raise more money for Sun's cause.

Except for the questions arising around Lin's age, no other inconsistencies with dates appear in the diary. In entries prior to this one, as with those that follow, dates always seem to coincide with actual events described. If we start with the assumption that the dates are correct, there is no reason to doubt Wong's description of his time spent with Sun Yat-sen. He quotes Dr. Sun about contemporary circumstances in China, writing that according to Sun, "Wan Siguay ... has built a powerful but corrupt army." The translation's spelling uses an older spelling for the name now more commonly spelled Yuan Shikai. In the spring of 1908, General Yuan was the most powerful military officer and politician in China and a principal advisor to the Dowager Empress Cixi. Sun appears to have shared his mistrust of Yuan with those who attended the 1908 New Westminster meeting. This mistrust would turn out to be well placed.

The winter 1908 entry begins with the news of the November 1908 death of Empress Cixi, which brought the young Emperor Puyi to the throne for three short years. His abdication on February 12, 1912, brought to an end both the Manchu Qing Dynasty and the two-thousand-year-old Imperial court of China. Dukesang Wong struggles over the next several years with the fading and eventual disappearance of the China that made him.

An almost thirty-month gap separates the last 1908 entry and the next entry in the early spring of 1911. New arrivals from China have met with Wong and his colleagues to hear their thoughts and opinions on the situation in the homeland, with the intention to pass those thoughts on to Sun Yat-sen. Wong writes honestly about his state of confusion. He seems unable to come to grips with the extraordinary change about to happen, a change from an "orderly" Imperial society, albeit one locked in virtual feudalism, to a modern republican democracy. The idea that the Imperial Court could end leaves him anxious and fearful for the lives that will be lost and the chaos that will follow.

A few months later his focus has returned to his family; Lin is pregnant with their sixth child. In the following two-sentence entry, Wong writes of learning about a "new governing order" devised by Sun Yat-sen. In all likelihood, Wong is referring to the Three Principles of the People, the elements of a hoped-for constitution first devised by Sun as early as 1905, but revised and developed by him over several years. An extremely simplified explanation of the Three Principles of the People defines them as nationalism, democracy, and socialism. The first principle proposed freeing the country of foreign influence, the second called for government for and by the people, and the third was a plan for social welfare and land reform. Both the Republic and the later People's Republic claimed the principles as the heart of their political philosophies.

Eight or nine months after the 1911 diary entries, the Wong family is celebrating the one-month birthday and official announcement of their sixth child, another son, as well as a good harvest and a homeland that is now a republic with elected representatives. Dukesang Wong continues to walk a thin line between celebration and regret, in part because he still believes men of reason could achieve the same result without armed revolution and the loss of life, and because he recognizes that with this literal transformation of his homeland, there is no longer any chance of restoring his father's name and reputation with the Imperial Court. He also makes another surprising mention of Sun Yat-sen. He claims that Sun promised to write with word about "our home villages." The identity of this "our" is a mystery, but unless it is a generalization referring to the home villages of all overseas Chinese, it once again suggests personal contact.

Sun Yat-sen was elected provisional President of the new Republic of China in 1911. Shortly thereafter, General Yuan Shikai manoeuvred himself into the presidency, replacing Sun in March 1912. Within a year Yuan had ordered the assassination of Song Jiaoren, the parliamentary leader of Sun's Kuomintang, the National People's Party. Sun called for a Second Revolution, this time against the autocratic Yuan, but was forced once again to flee to Japan. In 1914, Wong writes that Second Son[39] has taken "an avid interest in events happening in China." Was this new revolution the cause for which Second Son was "all in a fervour"? It is difficult to know, but in his concern for the boy, Wong writes of a "general arising from the peasantry" whose army was unruly, indiscriminately killing and stealing from the people in its path. He may well have been referring to Bai Lang and his army of bandits, deserting soldiers, revolutionaries, and criminals.[40] At its greatest strength, the army had several thousand members, and like Sun Yat-sen and his followers, their primary enemy was Yuan Shikai.

Many young men with a taste for revolution were drawn to the cause with little concern for the unruly reputation of Bai's army. Dukesang Wong would no doubt have been deeply disturbed at the prospect of his son's involvement. Nevertheless, within a matter of weeks, Second Son had departed Canada for China. Wong writes of his fear that he may never hear his son's laughter again, but as he has done before, he

---

39 Wong refers to his children by name only once in the diary, calling Second Son by his Chinese name, Sing. Wanda Joy knew him as Uncle Dan. Her other uncles were known to her as David, Charlie, Henry, and Harry. Her mother, Wong's only daughter, was called Elsie.

40 See Phil Billingsley, *Bandits in Republican China* (Stanford, CA: Stanford University Press, 1988).

takes an enlightened view of his children's decisions, suggesting that the search for knowledge outside the family home was to be encouraged.

Wong also expresses his pride in Third Son's commitment to helping the sick. In the autumn of the same year the young man entered university "in the eastern part of these lands." He had gone east to study medicine and eventually became a neurosurgeon.[41] Wong's one fear for Third Son, like Second Son, was also about war, although this time it was war in Europe that worried him. Although conscription was not imposed in Canada until 1917, arguments in favour of a draft would have begun earlier. Wong had seen many young men leave British Columbia for the battlefields of France, and he feared the same fate for his son. The final sentence of the 1914 entries, a little gem of philosophy and self-awareness, bears repeating. "It is said that the old ways cannot always last and that people must change and be continuously renewed. I have even taught this – yet I fear that I cannot change enough for this new world."

Two years on from that last thought, Wong writes that many of his people are travelling to Europe during the years of the First World War. According to him their primary purpose is to learn more about modern warfare and take that knowledge back to China, where it was sorely needed. For most of the nineteenth century, the Qing Dynasty armies had been woefully outclassed by the modern armies of colonial Europe and Japan. Attempts to modernize the Chinese military had been made under both Li Hongzhang and Yuan Shikai, but those attempts at modernization had limited results, and the divisive leadership of Yuan Shikai after 1913 finally led to what is now called the Warlord Era. In 1915, Yuan announced the establishment of a new "Empire of China," declaring himself Emperor. His "dynasty" lasted only eighty-three days before he was forced to abdicate and reaffirm the Republic. He died three months later, and the Warlord Era began. It was a time of lawlessness and constant warfare.

Sun Yat-sen returned from exile again in 1916 to lead his people in the effort to unify China. He did not live to see the unification he

---

41  In 1937, Third Son, known to Wanda Joy as Uncle David, became one of the founding doctors of Hong Kong's Queen Mary Hospital. He was joined soon after by his brother Henry, a pharmacologist, and his sister Elsie, a nurse and midwife. While serving at the hospital during World War II, Elsie met a wounded soldier who became her husband and Wanda Joy's father. After the war, they returned to Canada.

ardently believed would happen. He died of cancer in 1925. It would take several more years to train a National Army and over twenty years to subdue the regional warlords. "The turmoil within," which Wong wrote had "separated our people," may have referred to the revolution against Yuan, or to the struggles with the warlords after his death. In any event, western military techniques and instruments of war were much sought after by all parties in the many wars in China. It is not hard to imagine that for some, the battlefields and armaments factories of Europe were sources of much needed learning.

Dukesang Wong's eighth child and only daughter was born in 1918. Half a century later, his granddaughter, Wanda Joy, ended her university essay assignment with the diary entry that announced her mother's birth. There were other, later entries, but she chose not to translate them. With the birth of Wong's last child, the "Chinese Transition to Canada" was complete. Wong is at his most blatantly emotional in this 1918 entry, describing the birth as a "great joy" for the whole family. He admits to dabbling in both Buddhist and Christian ritual in having asked the deities to bless his family with a girl child. He relishes the love her seven brothers will show her as she grows and is greatly relieved that she will be there to look after Lin "when I leave these lands for the final journey homeward."

Though he anticipated his own death with those words, Dukesang Wong lived for another thirteen years, during which time he and Lin followed some of their adult children and relocated to the city of Vancouver, where Wong died in 1931 at the age of eighty-six. His body is interred in Vancouver's Mountain View Cemetery. The grave holds both his remains and those of his sixth son, Harry, who died the same year as his father. Nearby is the gravestone of his wife Lin-Ying, who lived to be one hundred. Her gravesite is shared with their only daughter, Wanda Joy's mother, Elsie. After graduating from university, Wanda Joy joined Canada's diplomatic service and served on the county's delegation to UNESCO in Paris, New York City, and Washington. Today Dukesang Wong has descendants living in cities around the world, including Vancouver, New York, London, Singapore, San Francisco, and Ottawa.

Fifty years ago, when she was translating selections from her grandfather's diary, Wanda Joy had no idea that what she recorded would turn out to be the sole extant voice to bear witness to the life and times of thousands of Chinese railway workers in Gold Mountain. She intended the story of her grandparent's transition to Canada, as told in the diaries, to be representative of thousands of families who left China both before and after the years of exclusion.[42] Her professor deemed it a perfectly relevant subject for a sociology assignment. We are often unsure why we keep some things and discard others, why we tuck a school essay in a cardboard box and store it for years in an attic or a garage. Whatever her reasons may have been, it is our very good fortune that Wanda Joy decided to do just that.

For most of a century, there was a collective forgetting about the significant Chinese contribution to settler history on the North American continent. That forgetting was exacerbated not only by racism and racist laws and by the denial of legitimacy, but also by the probable loss of first-person accounts of the Chinese experience. When Chinese buildings and their contents were destroyed, when the Chinese people were driven empty-handed from their homes, it surely meant the loss of at least a few notebooks, diaries, drawings, poems, and other personal observations. The Chinese version of the history of Gold Mountain was thought to have disappeared, with some relief from racist and anti-Chinese organizations, and the forgetting began. Several towns in both Canada and the United States, some of which had majority Chinese populations, began a whitewashing that is still evident today.

All of this is not to say that genuine efforts to acknowledge Chinese history in Canada and the U.S. have not been made. Communities have begun to correct their mistakes and apologize for the racism of the past, and perhaps these efforts will go some way to retrieving what has been forgotten. Dukesang Wong's diary – the diary of a Chinese railway worker, tailor, teacher, historian, philosopher, father, and grandfather – may also help to recover some of what has been lost. His observations begin with grieving his father's death and end by anticipating his own death half a century later, providing a valuable, first-person window onto our history. This entitled son of a magistrate of the Imperial Court of China had studied philosophy and history, and was on course to gain a position of authority and honour in service to the Qing dynasty, which would have numbered him among the Chinese mandarinate. However, that path evaporated, and a very different story unfolded instead – a fascinating story of two continents and two cultures, a personal and unique story that swept the man along in historic events, a Gold Mountain story we now know because, against all odds, he wrote it down.

---

42 1923–1947, when the Chinese Immigration Act banned almost all Chinese immigration to Canada.

# BIBLIOGRAPHY

Berton, Pierre. *The Last Spike: The Great Railway, 1881–1885.* Toronto, ON: Anchor Canada, 1971.

Billingsley, Phil. *Bandits in Republican China.* Stanford, CA: Stanford University Press, 1988.

Carlson, Keith Thor. "The Lynching of Louie Sam." *BC Studies* 109 (Spring 1996). ojs.library.ubc.ca/index.php/bcstudies/article /view/1309.

Chang, Iris. *The Chinese in America: A Narrative History.* New York: Penguin, 2004.

Chinese Reconciliation Project Foundation (website). "Expulsion: The Tacoma Method." www.tacomachinesepark.org/tacoma-chinese-park /expulsion-the-tacoma-method/.

Cornwall, Clement Francis, to the Secretary of State (Ottawa). Telegram. January 27, 1885. Library and Archives Canada, RG6-A-1, vol. 60, file 2235. Items 10–11.

Critical Thinking Consortium (TC²) (website). "Chinese Canadian Life on the Railway." tc2.ca/sourcedocs/uploads/history_docs/Chinese -Canadian%20History/Chinese-canadian-life-on-the-railway.pdf.

Daniels, Roger. *Asian America: Chinese and Japanese in the United States since 1850.* Seattle, WA: University of Washington Press, 1988.

Explore North: An Explorer's Guide to the North (website). "A History of BC's Fraser Canyon, 1808–1966." www.explorenorth.com/library /history/fraser_canyon-valley_of_death.html.

Foundation to Commemorate the Chinese Railroad Workers in Canada (website). "The Ties That Bind." www.mhso.ca/tiesthatbind /HeadTaxExclusion.php.

Government of Canada's Royal Commission on Chinese Immigration, with Sir Joseph-Adolphe Chapleau and John Hamilton Gray. *Report of the Royal Commission on Chinese Immigration: Report and Evidence.* Sessional Paper no. 54a. Ottawa, ON: Government of Canada's Royal Commission on Chinese Immigration, 1885. www.canadiana.ca/view/oocihm.14563/3?r=0&s=1.

Graybill, Andrew. "The Forgotten History of the Chinese Who Helped Build America's Railroads." *New York Times*, May 10, 2019. www.nytimes.com/2019/05/10/books/review/gordon-h-chang -ghosts-of-gold-mountain.html.

Hoe, Wanda Joy. "A Chinese Transition to Canada." Unpublished paper, 1966–1967.

Hummel, Arthur W., ed. *Eminent Chinese of the Ch'ing Period (1644–1912)*. Washington, DC: United States Government Printing Office, 1943.

Kōten, Rev. Master. "A History of Healing in Lytton." Lions Gate Buddhist Priory (website). www.lionsgatebuddhistpriory.ca/ARCHIVE%20 articles/NL98A.pdf.

Kwong, Peter, and Dušanka Miščević. *Chinese America: The Untold Story of America's Oldest New Community*. New York: New Press, 2007.

Lai, David Chuenyan. *Chinatowns: Towns within Cities in Canada*. Vancouver, BC: University of British Columbia Press, 2007.

Li, Peter S. *The Chinese in Canada*. Studies in Canadian Sociology series. Oxford, UK: Oxford University Press, 1998.

Luedi, Jeremy. "The Long Shadow of Canada's Chinese Head Tax." True North Far East (website). truenorthfareast.com/news /chinese-head-tax-canada-legacy.

Morton, James. *In the Sea of Sterile Mountains: The Chinese in British Columbia*, Vancouver, BC: J.J. Douglas, 1974.

Pan, Lynn, ed. *The Encyclopedia of the Chinese Overseas*. Cambridge, MA: Harvard University Press, 1998.

Roden, Barbara. "Golden Country: Past, Present, and Beyond: China-town." *Ashcroft-Cache Creek Journal*, August 23, 2016.

Statistics Canada. "Canada Year Book 1895." www66.statcan.gc.ca /eng/1895-eng.htm.

United States Department of the Interior. *Report of the Secretary of the Interior,* in *Message of the President of the United States and Accompanying Documents to the Two Houses of Congress at the Commencement of the First Session of the Thirty-Ninth Congress.* Washington, DC: U.S. Government Printing Office, 1865. books.google.ca /books?id=sEfg31gC6H4C&hl=fr&pg=PP21#v=onepage&q&f=false.

# ACKNOWLEDGMENTS

Wanda Joy Hoe translated selected excerpts from her grandfather's diary for a university essay and those translations are at the heart of this book. For that essay, "A Chinese Transition to Canada," for her blessing to make something from it, and for her memories, her encouragement, and her friendship, I am forever grateful to Wanda Joy and her family. Thanks to her son, Joshua Middleton, for his interest in his family's history and for his generous help.

For their early involvement I am grateful to Betsy Carson, Tracy Friesen, and especially to Yves Ma, whose guidance, friendship, and belief in this project often kept me going. Also to Li Xiao and Dylan Huang at the Shanghai Media Group, and to Bev Kennedy who opened a drawer and found the name Dukesang Wong. Thanks to my friend Colin Browne for his encouragement and for throwing me in the deep end. Howie Shia's drawings inspired me, and his observations were always on target. My gratitude to editors Catriona Strang and andrea bennett, whose commitment to the curious ways by which history emerges kept me digging and searching when I thought I was done.

I wrote this book for my daughter, Siena Xiao Di. And I couldn't have written it, or anything for that matter, without Rina Fraticelli in my life.

Born in a village north of Beijing, China, in 1845, **Dukesang Wong** travelled to North America in 1880 and worked for several years on the construction of the CPR in British Columbia. He eventually settled in New Westminster, BC, where he worked as a tailor and started a family. He died in 1931.

Born in 1947, **Wanda Joy Hoe** translated selections from the diary of her grandfather, Dukesang Wong, for an undergraduate sociology course at Simon Fraser University in the mid-1960s. After serving for many years with Canada's delegation to UNESCO, she retired and now lives in Ottawa.

**David McIlwraith** has been a writer, teacher, actor, and director. During a career in theatre, film, and television, he wrote and directed award-nominated documentaries and television programs, including *Celesta Found*, *The Lynching of Louie Sam*, *In Chinatown*, and *Harrowsmith Country Life*. He has worked across Canada in the development of new Canadian plays. As an actor, he has played roles from Romeo to Prospero, and he has taught at the University of Toronto and the University of Alberta. He spent a decade searching for and then researching this first-person account of the nineteenth-century Chinese experience in North America. He lives in Hamilton, Ontario, with his wife and daughter and spends summers with friends on Salt Spring Island.